VOCABBUSTERS GRE

VOCABBUSTERS GRE

Dusti D. Howell, Ph.D.
Deanne K. Howell, M.S.

Copyright © 2008 Dusti and Deanne Howell

Cartoon Copyright © 2004 Dusti and Deanne Howell

All rights reserved. No part of this book may be reproduced or utilized in any form or by any means, electronic or mechanical, including photocopying, recording, or by any information storage and retrieval system, without permission in writing from the publisher.

Pronunciation key and symbols reproduced by permission from Merriam-Webster's Online Dictionary at www.Merriam-Webster.com by Merriam-Webster, Incorporated.

ISBN 9780967732879

Printed in the United States of America

Authors:	Dusti D. Howell, Ph.D.
	Deanne K. Howell, M.S.
Illustrators:	James E. Rinehart II
	Brad Williams
Cover Design:	Another Design Guy, LLC
Book Layout:	Deanne Howell and Robert Reiter

SolidA, Inc.
Address:	1717 Sherwood Way
	Emporia, KS 66801
email:	info@solida.net
Internet:	http://www.solida.net

About the Authors

Dusti D. Howell, president of SolidA, has a Ph.D. in Educational Communications and Technology and a Ph.D. minor in Educational Psychology from the University of Wisconsin-Madison. Much of his research was done at Emporia State University as an Associate Professor in the Instructional Design and Technology Department. His expertise also includes innovations and research in high-tech study skills and digital learning strategies. Dusti has taught every grade level from first grade to graduate school.

Deanne K. Howell has earned a Masters Degree in Curriculum and Instruction from the University of Wisconsin-Madison. She is also an educator with experience teaching elementary through graduate classes.

Dusti and Deanne have published numerous books and articles, and have developed a number of workshops and multimedia programs.

SolidA, Inc. is dedicated to improving student learning with technology and scientific research. Our passion is to help learners succeed. Our goal is to help students get Solid A's.

Special Acknowledgments

We would like to express our sincere gratitude to:

Bob Reiter for his tireless work formatting the layout of this book.

Jim Rinehart and Brad Williams who brought humor and life to our words through their cartoon illustrations.

John C. Lehman, Communications Professor at Emporia State University, for generously donating his time and talent to the audio recordings.

Brenda Gray, for her work with the voice narrations.

Merriam-Webster, Incorporated for permission to use their written pronunciations throughout this book.

Julie Rosenquist and Ginger Lewman for their input and advise on this project.

We also thankful for Rachel Haskins and Cecelia White's assistance.

Table of Contents

Introduction 9
   Fun while learning vocabulary? 9
   Introducing the VOCABBUSTERS Methodology 9
   Why is having a good vocabulary important? 9
   VOCABBUSTERS is Simply the Best! 10
      1) Combining the Best Methods 10
         The Keyword Method 12
         Semantic-Context Method 12
      2) Study with Style 12
   VOCABBUSTERS caters to all types of learners 13
   Pronunciation Guide 15
      How to Review 15
   VOCABBUSTER Sample Overview 16
Section One 17
   Vocabulary Words 18
   Crossword Puzzle Review 38
   Multiple Choice Review 40
   Matching Review 42
Section Two 43
   Vocabulary Words 44
   Crossword Puzzle Review 64
   Multiple Choice Review 66
   Matching Review 68
Section Three 69
   Vocabulary Words 70
   Crossword Puzzle Review 90
   Multiple Choice Review 92
   Matching Review 94
Section Four 95
   Vocabulary Words 96
   Crossword Puzzle Review 116
   Multiple Choice Review 118
   Matching Review 120
Section Five 121
   Vocabulary Words 122
   Crossword Puzzle Review 142
   Multiple Choice Review 144

Section Six 147
    Vocabulary Words 148
    Crossword Puzzle Review 168
    Multiple Choice Review 170
    Matching Review 172
Section Seven 173
    Vocabulary Words 174
    Crossword Puzzle Review 194
    Multiple Choice Review 196
    Matching Review 198
Section Eight 199
    Vocabulary Words 200
    Crossword Puzzle Review 220
    Multiple Choice Review 222
    Matching Review 224
Section Nine 225
    Vocabulary Words 226
    Crossword Puzzle Review 246
    Multiple Choice Review 248
    Matching Review 250
Section Ten 251
    Vocabulary Words 252
    Crossword Puzzle Review 272
    Multiple Choice Review 274
    Matching Review 276
Free Resources 277
Example Sentence References 280
Bibliography 294
Answer Key 295
Index 300

Fun while learning vocabulary?

Vocabbusters introduces new words using a fun, multisensory approach.
* Each word is illustrated with a cartoon.
* Memory devices (mnemonics) are used to help you further remember and learn each word.
* Understand how each word is used in context with example sentences taken from major books and publications.
* Avoid mispronunciations by listening to the audio recordings.
* Enjoy watching select words come to life with clever animations that are sure to make you smile.
* Crossword puzzles, Matching Activies, and Multiple Choice Quizzes are included for review.
* Make up your own vocabulary cards by using the VOCABBUSTERS template at the back of this book.
* Learn how to search GoogleBooks to find your own words used in context.

For more free resources visit, http://www.solida.net

Introducing the VOCABBUSTERS Methodology

Learning vocabulary does not have to be difficult or dull. VOCABBUSTERS is based on over two decades of research on vocabulary acquisition, retention and usage. The strategies used in this book have been statistically proven to be superior learning devices for building vocabulary. VOCABBUSTERS combines two of the best methods to assist you in learning new words—the Keyword and Semantic-Context methods. The presentation of this information, centered on a cartoon, creates a memorable visual mnemonic. Audio recordings enable students to hear the words in order to pronounce the words correctly. Kinesthetic activities help to make learning easier and more fun.

Why is having a good vocabulary important?

Vocabulary acquisition is the single best indicator of intelligence and IQ according to Robert Sternberg, an Educational Psychologist at Yale University. Extensive portions of college entrance exams, including the S.A.T. and G.R.E., use vocabulary testing as a measure to predict academic performance. More importantly, simply reading does not guarantee a good vocabulary (Sternberg, 1986), which means that strategies for acquiring vocabulary need to be taught. Unfortunately, most schools do not devote any time for teaching effective techniques for learning vocabulary. When learning new vocabulary words, most students are left to rely on rote memorization, unaware that more efficient strategies are available. Therefore their vocabulary suffers, and in the end, many students remain ill prepared for college, and subsequently become more limited with their career choices.

VOCABBUSTERS is Simply the Best!

There are two simple reasons why VOCABBUSTERS is the best method for learning new vocabulary words. First, VOCABBUSTERS is two scientific methodologies built into one. By combining two of the most empirically validated methods for learning vocabulary into one simple interface, we have significantly increased the learner's chances for success. Second, we have added visual, auditory and kinesthetic supports to allow learners multiple "brain based" pathways for learning new words. That means you can study with just your strongest sensory style, or you can utilize all three sensory modalities. It all depends on what works best for you. For example, an auditory learner can just listen to the online audio files, or s/he can study the visual cartoons and easily utilize the kinesthetic techniques to quickly find dozens of example sentences online and then write a favorite one down at the bottom of each page. Again, our purpose is to easily provide the tools to allow you to study in the way that best suits your style of learning, thereby increasing your chances for success. Let's take a look at the two reasons why VOCABBUSTERS is the best in greater detail.

1) Combing the Best Methods

Numerous research articles have been written to prove the veracity of one method over another. It is interesting to note that in these "Battles of the Methods" two methods have been studied in great detail—the Keyword and Semantic-Context methods. In much of the research, the keyword method was shown to be very strong and empirically the best method for learning new vocabulary. However, over time, studies have shown semantic-context to be an excellent method, and in some cases as good as the keyword approach. A more detailed analysis of the strengths and weaknesses of each method led to an interesting discovery. The major strengths of each method complemented and added value to the other method. By juxtapositioning (combining) these two methods, the user will be able to easily remember definitions (keyword strength) and apply them in daily communications (semantic-context strength). For years these methods have been battling it out to see which one is the best. It is almost like comparing peanut butter and jelly. However, by combining the two methods into one new method, VOCABBUSTERS gives students a stronger base of research on which to rely.

The Keyword Method

The first step in using this method is to find a keyword for the word you are trying to learn. For example, let's say you're trying to learn the word *olfactory*. A good keyword for the word *olfactory* is *oil factory* because it follows three rules.

1. The word sounds acoustically similar to the target word.
2. The word is a concrete noun, which makes it easier to draw or visualize.
3. The word is common or familiar to the learner.

The second step is to link the keyword to the target definition. More simply, we need to link the word *oil factory* to "sense of smell." Visualize watching smoke spewing from an oil factory and smelling really bad. Draw a simple picture that depicts this situation and add the caption "That *oil factory* is bothering my *olfactory* sense." This visual mnemonic will assist the learner in remembering the meaning of the new word.

The final step is to practice recalling the target word. When you think of *olfactory*, first think of the keyword (*oil factory*), then remember what was happening in the picture (smoke is spewing out and smells bad), and finally that *olfactory* means *sense of smell.*

When tested against other methods, the keyword strategy repeatedly proved to be a superior technique for acquiring vocabulary for subjects of nearly all ages, and with periodic review, one of the best methods for long-term retention. The strength of this mnemonic strategy is in aiding the learner in remembering the definition of vocabulary words. Mnemonic strategies work! In fact, Purdue University researchers' Mastropieri and Scruggs (1991), "never found a 'type of learner' who could not benefit from mnemonic instruction." Additionally, the subjects in these studies not only liked the use of the strategy but expressed greater enjoyment in learning.

Semantic-Context Method

To learn a word using this method, context clues are placed in the sentence to help the learner define the word. For example, try to figure out what olfactory means from the following sentence. "His *olfactory* sense told him that someone had been smoking in the room." Clues within the sentence help the user define the meaning as "the sense of smell."

The semantic-context method has been identified as one of the best learning devices and has tested as one of the best strategies for delayed recall. Strictly speaking, in this book, only the first example sentence uses the semantic-context method. We created these sentences so that the target words were used within a meaningful context. We added two additional sentences from print sources that demonstrated real life examples. Although some of these sentences could also be considered semantic-context, only the first example sentence was strictly created for that purpose. These sentences as a whole should aid learners in actively integrating these words into their working vocabulary, using them on a daily basis.

2) Study with Style

What's your cognitive style? Do you learn best when you see an illustration depicting the meaning of a new word (visual), when you hear the new word being used (auditory), or when you find an example of the word used in real life and write it down (kinesthetic)? By providing visual cartoons, audio narrations and kinesthetic activities, we allow users to study with their primary learning styles. Keyword mnemonics create excellent visual links connecting keywords to the definitions of the targeted vocabulary word. This visual approach is best for recalling word definitions. We created the audio from the caption sentences of the cartoons and from each semantic-context sentence (first example sentence for each word). Auditory learners should find these extremely helpful in learning these words. Finally, kinesthetic learners can follow the directions on page fourteen to quickly find dozens of example sentences online and then write a favorite one down at the bottom of each page.

Many will certainly find it useful to integrate all three of these approaches into the learning process for each word. By listening to the recordings while reading over the sentences and studying the cartoon, and then searching through lists of example sentences and selecting one to write down, users will be storing this information in multiple locations of their brain. Proponents of dual coding theory claim that multimedia enhanced lessons can help strengthen the learning process by processing the same information in multiple areas of the brain, including the visual and auditory cortexes. Even more than dual coding, perhaps those that use all three approaches are using triple coding. Either way, every one of these supports is given with the goal of giving learners multiple methods to succeed.

VOCABBUSTERS Caters to all Types of Learners.

Here's how VOCABBUSTERS engages the three primary senses in learning new words.

What's Your Cognitive Style?
Find out free at www.solida.net

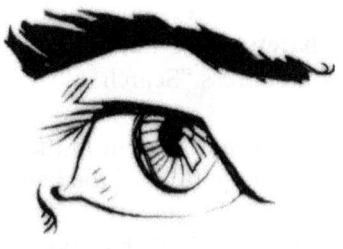

Visual Learners learn best when they see a visual image or picture. The cartoon illustrations for each word create a humorous and memorable way for learning new words. When trying to recall the meaning of a word, visual learners should try to remember the keyword and the related cartoon that illustrates the word. Recalling the activity in the cartoon helps visual learners remember the meaning of the target word. Additionally, visual learners might find it beneficial to color the pictures in the book.

Auditory Learners - Audio files increase learning and eliminate the guess work from determining pronunciations. Students no longer need to worry about whether they are mispronouncing words. According to middle school teacher Ginger Lewman, "I've had kids work on words by themselves and come back to

me mispronouncing them. For instance, the word facade (pronounced f&-'säd) becomes f&-'kAd. Now that could be VERY embarrassing on down the road and discourage them from trying to learn new words on their own." With the audio recordings, auditory learners can easily learn new words independently and pronounce them correctly. Students with auditory preferences can review words by listening to them at any time.

Watch and listen to select words come to life in funny animated cartoons at http://www.solida.net.

Kinesthetic Learners- Interact with the words by creating additional example sentences for each word. A great way to do this is to use *Google Books*. Google Books is a completely free online search engine that enables users to search inside books for pages that include a particular word. Here's how to use this valuable tool:

1. Go to Google's Books website at http://books.google.com.
2. If you are searching for the word **baleful**, type **baleful** in the Google Search Books window and press "Search Books."
3. Pick your favorite sentence from this list and write it in the "write your own" section provided at the bottom of the page.

Use the VOCABBUSTERS template at the back of this book to make your own "VOCABBUSTERS" or visit www.solida.net to print it from a PDF file.

For additional kinesthetic activities solve the crossword puzzles and take the matching and multiple choice quizzes at the end of the chapters. Also try to Listen to the MP3 recordings while moving about.

Pronunciation Guide

Many words have more than one correct pronunciation. In this book we have included one or two of the most common pronunciations for each word.

(http://www.m-w.com/cgi-bin/dictionary#)

\ə\ as **a** and **u** in **a**b**u**t	\ᵊ\ as **e** in kitt**e**n	\ər\ as **ur/er** in f**ur**th**er**
\a\ as **a** in **a**sh	\A\ as **a** in **a**ce	\ä\ as **o** in m**o**p
\au\ as **ou** in **ou**t	\ch\ as **ch** in **ch**in	\e\ as **e** in b**e**t
\E\ as **ea** in **ea**sy	\g\ as **g** in **g**o	\i\ as **i** in h**i**t
\I\ as **i** in **i**ce	\j\ as **j** in **j**ob	\[ng]\ as **ng** in si**ng**
\O\ as **o** in g**o**	\o\ as **aw** in l**aw**	\oi\ as **oy** in b**oy**
\th\ as **th** in **th**in	\[th]\ as **th** in **th**e	\ü\ as **oo** in l**oo**t
\u\ as **oo** in f**oo**t	\y\ as **y** in **y**et	\zh\ as **si** in vi**si**on

By permission of the publisher. From Merriam-Webster's Online Dictionary at www.merriam-webster.com by Merriam-Webster, Incorporated.

How to Review

Try to recall as much information about each word before looking at the page. You may wish to cover up the page, with only the target vocabulary word visible. Try to recall each part before uncovering it. To review the word *olfactory*:

1. Recall the keyword [oil factory]
2. Visualize the cartoon picture of the sun inhaling the fumes from the smelly oil factory.
3. Connect the picture to the meaning of the target word [referring to the sense of smell]
4. Think about how the word was used in a sentence or try to make up a sentence of your own.

VOCABBUSTERS Sample Overview

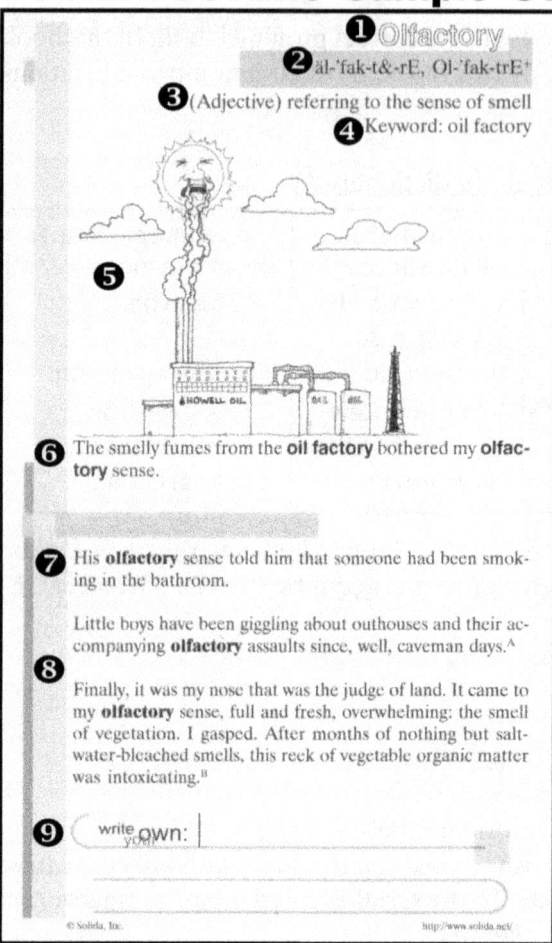

1. Target word
2. Pronunciations are from the experts at Merriam-Webster. Many words have more than one pronunciation.
3. Part of speech and definition.
4. The keyword consists of a word or short phrase that sounds similar to the target word.
5. Cartoon illustration links the target word to the keyword and definition.
6. The cartoon caption ties the target word to the keyword and definition.
7. The target word used within a meaningful sentence (Semantic Context).
8. Two example sentences taken from leading books or publications.
9. Create your own sentence using the target word. Use the directions on page xii to find great example sentences.

Section One

Abet

'&-'bet

(Verb) to actively aid or help (usually in some wrongdoing)
Keyword: a bet

By distracting the dealer, the cheater **abetted** his buddy in stealing a few coins during **a bet**.

Camille wisely refused to **abet** her friends in shoplifting.

In the story ... a wacky cast of estate workers and locals ... aid and **abet** the conspiracies, disasters and love affairs of the family.[3]

[In the human body] redundant mechanisms have evolved to ensure that fuel is conserved as fat to **abet** survival in lean times....[4]

write your own:

Abeyance

&-'bA-&nts or &-'bA-&ns

(Noun) a temporary suspension (interruption) of function or activity
Keyword: advance

The runners were held in **abeyance** and were not allowed to **advance** due to the construction of the bridge.

The dance was held in **abeyance**--temporarily postponed until a band could be found.

Summer is finally a-coming in, just in time for the annual open-air symphony concerts. In Melbourne, this tradition has been in **abeyance** for two years while the Sidney Myer Music Bowl has been refurbished [restored or fixed up]....[1]

She has created a few areas in which she lets go of that practical, conservative side, in particular a lifelong love of sports cars (currently in **abeyance** with a city-owned car and family minivan).[2]

write your own: _____

Abrogate

'a-br&-"gAt

(Verb) to end; to abolish formally, or to officially get rid of

Keyword: afro date

The afro date law requiring all students to have an **afro** hair style in order to **date** was **abrogated** after several new bald students came to the school.

In an attempt to **abrogate** all speeding, the local police force was heavily patrolling all the streets in our town.

It is not fair to hold every parent responsible for a child's misfortunes, but neither can a parent **abrogate** his or her protective role....[5]

There really was a Sheriff of Nottingham, though: his name, Philip Mark, even appears in the Magna Carta, a landmark document drawn up by rebellious lords seeking to **abrogate** the absolute power of tyrants [all powerful rulers] like Philip's employer, King John.[6]

write your own:

Abstruse

&b-'strüs or ab-'strüs

(Adjective) difficult to comprehend; obscure
Keyword: abscessed tooth

With an **abscessed tooth**, the professor's **abstruse** lecture became even more difficult to understand.

The physics professor had a way of making **abstruse** concepts simple and easy to understand.

Breaking news from the world of particle physics tends to be greeted with a great big "Huh?" ... Theories of how the tiniest bits of matter and energy interact left the realm of common sense decades ago and are now wrapped up in **abstruse** mathematics and mind-bending terminology.[7]

Understanding the concept is not all that difficult. It's the math part ... that makes it all seem so **abstruse**.[8]

write your own:

Alacrity

&-'la-kr&-tE

(Noun) cheerful readiness or willingness; responding promptly
Keyword: a lack of tea

When there was **a lack of tea**, the guests accepted the offer of coffee with great **alacrity**.

After winning the lottery, Darin accepted the significant sum of cash with great **alacrity**.

The film, which focused on the work of the Red Cross, captured [Princess] Diana's imagination and she agreed with **alacrity** to help raise funds in the campaign to rid the world of landmines.[11]

Dog owners have taken to the target stick with **alacrity**. One can use a target stick to teach a rambunctious, out-of-control

write your own:

Amalgamate

&-'mal-g&-"mAt

(Verb) to unite or join into one
(especially groups or organizations)
Keyword: animal gate

The zoo animals had to **amalgamate** into one group at feeding time to go through the **animal gate**.

The school dropped its band program and **amalgamated** its members into the orchestra when they lost their band leader.

He declined to approve the charter granted by Dongan, and at once sought to **amalgamate** all of the colonies north and east of the Delaware River into a dominion of New England.[17]

The tomb's peculiar form may have resulted from an attempt to **amalgamate** the architectural features of three different civilizations....[18]

write your own:

Amiable

'A-mE-&-b&l

(Adjective) friendly; agreeable
Keyword: Amy's stable

At **Amy's stable**, all of the horses are **amiable** and friendly.

Although Kristin is generally **amiable**, she can be unpleasant when she has not had enough sleep.

Doss is an **amiable**, soft-spoken, extremely thoughtful man....[21]

Parrots can be unpredictable. One generally **amiable** sulphur-crested Cockatoo named Tommy ... took umbrage when a friend of his owner began to wear glasses. After due reflection, he reached up and bit the man on the lip.[22]

write your own:

Anomaly

&-'nä-m&-lE

(Noun) someone or something that is uncommon or irregular
Keyword: anemone

The discovery of the sea **anemones** was an **anomaly** in the fresh water lake.

Scientists had performed the experiment repeatedly with the same results, but this time something was different. The results were an **anomaly**.

The vampire bats are pretty darn cool, the exotic birds are beautiful, and the guy in the scuba gear cleaning the tank was an interesting **anomaly**, looking klutzy among more graceful (albeit confined) creatures.[19]

His pediatrician picked up an **anomaly** in his heart during a routine checkup. The cardiologist confirmed that [he] had several holes in his heart.[20]

write your own: _____

_____

Apocryphal

&-'pä-kr&-f&l

(Adjective) false; not genuine
Keyword: a pocket full

The young boy had **a pocket full** of **apocryphal** diamonds which he sold to his classmates, even though they were fake.

Many urban legends are spread via email. These **apocryphal** hoaxes can quickly be debunked at an urban legend website.

Preparing us against snakebite, Japper had brought a battery-powered cattle prod. If applied quickly, he said, the electrical shock would mitigate [minimize] the effect of a bite. Fortunately we never had to test this **apocryphal** snakebite remedy.[23]

When the Lutheran minister came to his house in St. Louis to recruit my grandmother, he beat him up. Maybe it's an **apocryphal** family legend....[24]

write your own:

Arbiter

'är-b&-t&r

(Noun) a person who mediates or judges
Note: same as arbitrator
Keyword: orbiter

An **arbiter** was hired to mediate all of the disputes between the astronauts on the **orbiter**.

Because the two students could not talk to each other without getting into a fight, the teacher served as an **arbiter** while they discussed their problems.

A new exhibition of the royal wardrobe, to which the queen has given her blessing, pays homage to the accessories that have won her acclaim from many **arbiters** of style....[27]

He dominated all aspects of [the city's] public life, and he was the final **arbiter** of virtually every piece of government policy.[28]

write your own:

Assiduous

&-'sij-w&s   or   &-'si-j&-w&s

(Adjective) persistent; diligent; constant attention
Keyword: acid

To determine the effects of acid on limestone, the scientist had the **assiduous** task of adding **acid** to the limestone every half hour for two weeks.

The college students were **assiduous** in their year long fight for better food in the cafeteria.

[Thomas] Jefferson described [Meriwether Lewis] as "an **assiduous** and attentive farmer, observing with minute attention all plants and insects he met with."[27]

Grimm is clearly an **assiduous** scholar of Elizabethan literary language, and he mimics it with impressive determination.[28]

write your own:

Attenuation

&-"ten-y&-'wA-sh&n

(Noun) the act of making thinner, smaller or weaker
Keyword: a tent station

Due to the **attenuated** budget for the radio station, the D.J. saved money by working in **a tent station** in his backyard.

The hikers were shocked at the **attenuation** of their food supply after only three days of camping.

During that time, Pasteur enhanced the concept of **attenuation**, which is the use of a weakened form of a virus to provide immunity. Pasteur found that a weakened form of chicken cholera (an **attenuated** form) was highly effective in preventing the disease. **Attenuated** vaccines are widely used today.[29]

Indeed, it is not unknown for the shade temperature in the city to be a little lower than in the surrounding countryside ... because of the slight **attenuation** of the city sunlight by the dust and smoke endemic [prevalent in] in the urban atmosphere.[30]

write your own: _____

http://SolidA.net

Audacious

o-'dA-sh&s

(Adjective) bold or adventurous
Keyword: all day shifts

The **audacious** mountain rescue job required workers to be able to handle **all day shifts**, 24 hours straight, under the worst of conditions.

Though Bill's **audacious** idea was initially dismissed as being too bold and dangerous, his friends started to come around later.

The proposal was **audacious** — the New Orleans Saints offering to trade all of their 1999 draft picks, plus future considerations, for the chance to select Heisman Trophy-winning running back Ricky Williams of Texas.[33]

Days of **audacious** daylight robberies, thwarted by Marines, have left two blocks of the district a gutted [looted] ruin.[34]

write your own:

Aver

&-'v&r

(Verb) to verify or confirm the truth
Keyword: love her

He was finally able to **aver** his **love** to **her**, when he proposed marriage.

After being accused of breaking the window, the child **averred** and apologized for throwing the ball.

The black huckleberry ... is the most popular, but Fernald and Kinsey **aver** that the dangleberry ... is just as good and will make one of the most luscious of deserts, being remarkably juicy and with a rich spicy flavor.[35]

Akagi's log (journal) **avers** that she saw the attackers fifty kilometers out.[36]

write your own: _____

Baleful

'bAl-f&l or bA&l-f&l

(Adjective) harmful, with evil intention
Keyword: bale full

With **baleful** intent, Roger placed sneezing powder in the **bale full** of hay to make the cows miserable.

Her **baleful** stares sent shivers throughout my body. I could detect the evil intentions and the hatred in her eyes.

Martin Gilbert, the assiduous historian of Nazi crimes, turns in "The Righteous" toward the better side of the story, the record of those virtuous men and women who came to the rescue of Jews in the **baleful** years of 1940-45.[35]

The big lynx was not cooperating. Tipped gently from his metal crate onto a meadow near the Rio Grande Reservoir, he cast a **baleful** look at the people chattering in front of him—and growled.[36]

write your own:

Bane

'bAn

(Noun) the cause of injury or mischief
Keyword: brain

The cigarette smoke was a **bane** to his **brain**, and gave him the worst headache.

Fans who don't want to pay for CDs or MP3s anymore are the current **bane** of the music industry.

The disruption of your body's sleep cycle after along transcontinental flight-better known as jet lag-is the **bane** of every business traveler.[37]

Economically, we are the **bane**, not the hope of the world. Since the planet is finite [limited], as we expand our economy we make it less likely that less developed nations can expand theirs.[38]

write your own: _____

Belie

bi-'lI

(Verb) to misrepresent or expose something as false
Keyword: bee lied

The **bee lied** to the bear, in order to **belie** the vast amount of honey to be found in the hive.

All the beauty pageant contestants had calm and collected looks on their faces that **belied** the nervousness and excitement they were feeling before the winner was announced.

Greenville's small size and low-key attitude **belie** a thriving business center with a flourishing downtown....[37]

Tampa Bay Buccaneers coach Jon Gruden knows one effect of his addiction to coaching: those bags under his eyes that **belie** the fact he won't turn 40 until this summer.[38]

write your own:

Bellicose

'be-li-"kOs

(Adjective) warlike or aggressive
Keyword: bells in clothes

The eerie sound of the **bells in clothes** could be heard as the **bellicose** invaders marched closer.

Some of the child's actions and statements were so **bellicose** that his parents were forced to have the child see a counselor before he attacked someone.

One afternoon he was riding home on a suburban Tokyo train when a huge, **bellicose**, and very drunk laborer got on. The man began terrorizing the passengers: screaming curses....[39]

So the writer has to take the most used, most familiar objects; nouns, pronouns, verbs, adverbs, ...and make people get into a romantic mood; and another way, into a **bellicose** mood.[40]

write your own:

Bemuse

bi-'myüz

(Verb) to confuse or stupefy/ absorb in thought
Keyword: be a moose

The park ranger was **bemused** to learn that he would have to **be a moose** to follow the migratory patterns of the herd.

I was **bemused** by Lisa's sudden rage at me. I thought we were friends.

You can park overnight for free at a gas station by putting a note under your wiper that says you broke down and have gone for help. Usually, people break down and walk to a gas station, so this reversal of logic will baffle and **bemuse** the attendants. [42]

Allende knows that the view she offers is hazy, but she wants it that way. Her aim in this nonfiction memoir of the spirits is not to clarify but to obscure, to emphasize and, as she says, to invent her native country so as to **bemuse** us. [41]

write your own:

Bereft

bi-'reft

(Adjective) being without something that is needed or wanted
Keyword: theft

The museum was **bereft** of many artifacts and looked strangely empty after the **theft**.

Phillip stood frozen in front of his class, **bereft** of words, after he was asked to give an impromptu speech.

Without assistance, African governments cannot afford spraying programs [to kill mosquitoes], leaving them **bereft** of a safe, effective, and cheap defense [from malaria].[41]

Bereft of good leadership, they are trapped in needless bickering....[42]

write your own:

Section 1 Crossword Puzzle

Across

3. friendly; agreeable
5. being without something that is needed or wanted
6. a temporary suspension of function or activity
10. to actively aid or help (usually in some wrongdoing)
11. difficult to comprehend; obscure
12. persistent; diligent; constant attention
13. to unite or join into one (especially groups or organizations)
16. cheerful readiness or willingness; responding promptly
17. to verify or confirm the truth

Down

1. a person who mediates or judges
2. to misrepresent or expose something as false
4. the cause of injury or mischief
5. to confuse or stupefy/ absorb in thought
6. someone or something that is uncommon or irregular
7. false; not genuine
8. harmful, with evil intention
9. warlike or aggressive
12. the act of making thinner, smaller, or weaker
14. to end; to abolish formally or to officially get rid of
15. bold or adventurous

Section 1 Multiple Choice Review

Select the word that best fits each sentence.

1. After her dog passed away, Pam felt utterly _____ and lonely.
   a. belied   b. bereft   c. averred   d. baleful

2. The _____ lawyer worked tirelessly for two months in order to prepare his defense.
   a. bemused   b. apocryphal   c. audacious   d. assiduous

3. The mere title of the book Michelle found at the library was so _____ that she had no clue what it was about.
   a. bereft   b. baleful   c. amiable   d. abstruse

4. As part of a large renovation process taking place at the university, four different offices will be _____ into one main office that will serve the students' needs more efficiently.
   a. abetted   b. amalgamated   c. abrogated   d. belied

5. It is no wonder Samuel is spending the rest of his life in jail, with the _____ influence of his friends, he didn't have much of a chance.
   a. abstruse   b. amalgamated   c. baleful   d. bane

6. The tradition of eating turkey on Thanksgiving in my family was _____ after my parents became vegetarians.
   a. abrogated   b. averred   c. apocryphal   d. abetted

7. Many news reports _____ what is really going on in some foreign countries.
   a. belie   b. abet   c. amalgamate   d. abeyance

8. Dena drove to the airport with great _____ because she was so excited to see her friend after being apart for three years.
   a. abeyance   b. alacrity   c. attenuation   d. audacity

9. After incorrectly being accused of cheating, the student _____ that the answers were his own by showing his worksheet.
   a. averred   b. abrogated   c. attenuated   d. bemused

10. Sandy _____ her friends in the bank robbery by driving them to the bank.
    a. bemused   b. belied   c. amalgamated   d. abetted

11. Attempting to start a water balloon fight, Jerry made some _____ comments that would entice his hopeful opponents to participate.
    a. bellicose   b. amiable   c. bereft   d. assiduous

12. While waiting to find out if she got the part in the play, Amy tried to keep her nervousness in _____.
    a. abeyance   b. alacrity   c. bane   d. attenuation

13. Because the new employee wore such crazy clothes, he was considered a(n) _____ in the office.
    a. bane   b. anomaly   c. arbiter   d. abrogate

14. Though many of the stories passed down in my family have always been held to be true, if any research is done on them they will probably be found to be _____.
    a. bellicose   b. audacious   c. apocryphal   d. assiduous

15. Charlie strongly disliked Pedro, but both boys were surprisingly _____ during the picnic.
    a. baleful   b. amiable   c. abstruse   d. audacious

16. The prisoners planned a(n) _____ escape that cut through the adjoining guard station.
    a. assiduous   b. averred   c. bellicose   d. audacious

17. Experiencing frequent migraines is the _____ of my existence.
    a. bane   b. anomaly   c. alacrity   d. aversion

18. When I inquired about the incident, John's _____ look immediately indicated that he had nothing to do with what happened.
    a. arbiter   b. amiable   c. bellicose   d. bemused

19. Jane was the _____ for her siblings and tried to help them resolve their arguments before her mother got involved.
    a. bane   b. abrogate   c. arbiter   d. amalgamate

20. By dropping two classes, the student felt less stressed due to her _____ class load.
    a. attenuated   b. abrogated   c. anomalous   d. apocryphal

Section 1 Matching Review

Directions: Match each word with its correct meaning.

1. ____ Abet
2. ____ Abeyance
3. ____ Abrogate
4. ____ Abstruse
5. ____ Alacrity
6. ____ Amalgamate
7. ____ Amiable
8. ____ Anomaly
9. ____ Apocryphal
10. ____ Arbiter
11. ____ Assiduous
12. ____ Attenuation
13. ____ Audacious
14. ____ Aver
15. ____ Baleful
16. ____ Bane
17. ____ Belie
18. ____ Bellicose
19. ____ Bemuse
20. ____ Bereft

A. to unite or join into one (especially groups or organizations)
B. warlike or aggressive
C. to end; to abolish formally or to officially get rid of
D. to misrepresent or expose something as false
E. a temporary suspension of function or activity
F. the act of making thinner, smaller, or weaker
G. being without something that is needed or wanted
H. harmful, with evil intention
I. bold or adventurous
J. to actively aid or help (usually in some wrongdoing)
K. cheerful readiness or willingness; responding promptly
L. someone or something that is uncommon or irregular
M. friendly; agreeable
N. a person who mediates or judges
O. persistent; diligent; constant attention
P. false; not genuine
Q. to verify or confirm the truth
R. to confuse or stupefy/ absorb in thought
S. the cause of injury or mischief
T. difficult to comprehend; obscure

Section Two

Bombastic

bäm-'bas-tik

(Adjective) using words that sound important in order to appear smarter
Keyword: bomb blast

The **bomb blast** expert's news conference sounded impressive, although no one understood his **bombastic** speech.

The **bombastic** preacher used Greek and Hebrew words throughout his sermon to try to increase his credibility.

I could have said that he was **bombastic** and loved the sound of his own voice, but that was not true.[45]

The second source of fury is the authors' **bombastic** style in describing power lawyers. A few examples will suffice: "twin towers of ambition and acquisitiveness," "supportive of the employer's macho-militant posture," "well-paid peddlers of influence."[46]

write your own:

Boor

'bur

(Noun) a person lacking manners or taste;
a rude person
Keyword: burr

After stepping on the pokey **burrs** with her barefoot, Sally became such a **boor** that no one wanted to help her remove them.

David was considered a **boor** because of his tactless habit of speaking his mind and offending others.

The guy comes off as one insufferable, egotistical **boor**.[47]

George II is generally seen as a headstrong, blinkered [narrow-minded] **boor**, manipulated in his early years as king by his wife, Queen Caroline and by his chief minister….[48]

write your own:

Broach

'brOch

(Verb) to open up; to mention a subject
Keyword: roach

After a **roach** was discovered in the restaurant kitchen, it was necessary to **broach** the topic of sanitation with the manager.

The room immediately fell silent when the sensitive subject that no one had yet dared to **broach** was finally brought up.

Yvonne has decided to **broach** the subject with Jotham. Rather than waiting until they're both upset, she's picked a time when they're relaxing on the couch.[49]

Some social democrats are also beginning to **broach** what has long been considered a taboo subject among their faithful.[50]

write your own:

Cacophony

ka-'kä-f&-nE or ka-'ko-f&-nE

(Noun) a harsh assortment of loud and unpleasant sounds
Keyword: cough funny

"You **cough funny**!" exclaimed Bob as his friend coughed and disturbed the library with a loud **cacophony** of harsh sounds.

The elementary band sounded more like a **cacophony** of random sounds, rather than music.

The arena's in-house restaurant and bar filled with a **cacophony** of noise when, on the television screens overhead, unheralded [unpredicted] Los Angeles Kings forward Mikko Eloranta scored on Dan Cloutier of Vancouver...[49]

Amid the dusty bedlam [chaos] of Kathmandu's neighborhood, [was] a **cacophony** of motorcycle engines, truck horns, rooster calls, police whistles, fruit hawkers, and chanting sidewalk monks fill the kerosene-laced air....[50]

write your own: _____

Candor

'kan-d&r or 'kan-"dor

(Noun) truthfulness or sincerity

Keyword: canned dirt

The company confessed with **candor** that the idea to market **canned dirt** was bad.

The parent was able to talk about his child's misbehavior with more **candor** than the school administration would have expected.

When Duke University surgeons last month transplanted an incompatible set of organs into [the] teenager ... who would later die, the doctors and hospital publicly confessed the mix-up and apologized. Such **candor** is part of a growing trend among hospitals to own up to the truth when patients are harmed....[51]

It is clear that after Ford was named vice president, a change came over his wife. Slowly, she [Betty Ford] was beginning to revert back to the woman she had been before she married Gerald Ford-a self-assured woman of **candor** who enjoyed the spotlight.[52]

write your own:

Capitulate

k&-'pi-ch&-"lAt

(Verb) to accept defeat unwillingly
Keyword: capture bait

The **captured bait capitulated** after the fisherman dug them up and ordered them to go to the bait stand.

Stephanie finally **capitulated** to the constant pleading of her friends and left her studies for a trip to the lake.

Motivated by love of his daughter and her future he **capitulates**, surrendering his own beliefs for her hopes.[57]

The fight for Baghdad could be more like a siege than a battle unless the Iraqis **capitulate** or President Bush changes his stated goals....[58]

write your own:

Capricious

k&-'pri-sh&s or k&-'prE-sh&s

(Adjective) unpredictable, whimsical, or impulsive
Keyword: cup of fishes

Because the **capricious** children could not decide on a fish to buy, the pet store owner gave them a **cup of fishes** to take home.

The mother was unable to please her **capricious** daughter, who always wanted a different toy.

It is generally agreed that the weather of spring is not to be relied upon. Or, to put it another way, it is to be relied upon— to be utterly **capricious**, mean and nasty one moment, smiles and sweetness the next, like little girls.[53]

It is possible for the lady to be hostile, fiercely independent, passive, feminine, aggressive and warm. Of course at any particular moment would not be **capricious**— it would depend on who she is with, when, how, and much more.[54]

write your own:

Castigate

'kas-t&-"gAt

(Verb) to punish or criticize harshly
Keyword: cast on a gate

The doctor **castigated** the patient for fooling around and ultimately breaking his **cast on a gate**.

After the accident, the owner of the amusement park was **castigated** for not meeting the safety regulations.

Unlucky persons are likely to **castigate** themselves with thoughts of "This need not have happened" or "I brought this on myself."[55]

It is easy to point at the public offender and **castigate** him in shame and judgment.[56]

write your own: _____

Chagrin

sh&-'grin

(Noun) distress or embarrassment caused by failure

Keyword: share a grin

Much to the actor's **chagrin**, the audience **shared a grin** when she accidentally tripped and fell on stage.

Imagine my **chagrin** when I realized that I had driven 200 miles in the wrong direction.

Years later, when Franklin was a world-famous figure, and Ambassador to France, he still remembered that the fact that he had paid too much for his whistle had caused him "more **chagrin** than the whistle gave him pleasure."[61]

[He] managed to pull in a 6-pound northern pike just 45 minutes after leaving the docks at 5 a.m., much to the **chagrin** of his wife [who perhaps had to cook it].[62]

write your own:

Cognizant

'käg-n&-z&nt

(Adjective) having knowledge of something; informed
Keyword: cog is bent

The wheel maker is **cognizant** of the fact that the **cog is bent** and is in need of repair.

The children were not **cognizant** that a big surprise was planned for them and waiting just around the corner.

Rather than just we veterans, everyone is more **cognizant** of what Memorial Day means this year....[59]

Scott's wife and children know better than to interrupt the Nets' coach when he's scouting potential opponents for next week's conference finals.—"Everybody else will be wherever they've got to be, but it won't be in there with me," Scott said yesterday... "I'm watching it as a fan, but also as a coach, trying to be **cognizant** of what's going on."[60]

write your own:

Conciliatory

k&n-'sil-y&-"tOr-E

(Adjective) attempting to unite or win over

Keyword: one silly story

Instead of fighting, the general's **conciliatory** approach is to win over his enemies by telling **one silly story**.

The union's **conciliatory** gesture broke the stalemate [standstill] and allowed the negotiations to continue on more friendly terms.

Wilson's antiwar and anti-imperialist secretary of state, William Jennings Bryan, was inclined to be **conciliatory** toward Germany in order to avoid war.[63]

Roosevelt actually pursued what amounted to a stalling strategy in Asia for months, alternating economic embargoes [trade stoppages] with **conciliatory** negotiations.[64]

write your own:

Contumacious

"kän-tü-'mA-sh&s"

(Adjective) insubordinate, rebellious, or disobedient
Keyword: cons' tune

The **cons' tune** included rebellious lyrics that sounded too **contumacious** to the prison guards.

The **contumacious** child refused to obey his parents.

You've been "conserving" calories for years—with diet sodas, low-fat milk and lately with fat-free potato chips. Yet your **contumacious** scale simply refuses to acknowledge the facts.[69]

"No," replied the captain, "but we must warn your Excellency that the island is **contumacious**."
"What do you mean?"
"That Monte Cristo, although uninhabited, yet serves occasionally as a refuge for the smugglers and pirates...." [70]

write your own: _____

Conundrum

k&-'n&n-dr&m

(Noun) a question or riddle that is difficult to solve
Keyword: con and drum

Sherlock Holmes was brought in to solve the **conundrum** of the escaped **con and drum**.

Newlyweds are often faced with the **conundrum** of whose parents to visit during the holidays.

Countless scientific, technological and economic issues affect our understanding of the climate **conundrum** and our response to it.[67]

Since the book's launch in 2000, RS's fashion pages have been a **conundrum** for its two previous editors. Finding the right balance between sensible and stylish clothes has not been easy.[68]

write your own:

Countermand

'kaun-t&r-"mand or "kaun-t&r-'mand

(Verb) to annul; cancel/ make a contrary order
Keyword: counter man

Although the king's **counter man** was accurate, the king **countermanded** his total because he wanted to appear richer.

The substitute teacher **countermanded** all of our teacher's previous rules and allowed us total freedom in the classroom.

I've made up my mind, and none of you have the rank to **countermand** my order.[71]

Other Bush advisers say he might use a nonconfrontational approach to reach his goal—delay implementation of some of Clinton's recent initiatives … until he believes the moment is right to **countermand** them permanently.[72]

write your own: _____

Craven

'krA-v&n

(Adjective) cowardly; extreme defeatism and complete lack of resistance
Keyword: raven

The **craven raven** was too afraid to eat the food from the boy's hand.

Given her **craven** attitude, Sue's friends were sure that she would never go skydiving with them.

To someone who hasn't been through a decision so fraught with conflict this must sound ridiculous, confused, irrational, and **craven**.[73]

No warrior with any concept of honor would have been so **craven**.[74]

write your own:

Credulous

'kre-j&-l&s

(Adjective) gullible; too trusting; ready to believe especially on slight or uncertain evidence
Keyword: credit [card]

The **credulous** woman handed her **credit card** to the crook who told her he needed it to make a payment on his emergency heart transplant.

Although normally quite **credulous**, Dustin refused to believe a word of what his co-workers were telling him this time.

But then it was, as we should not forget, an altogether more **credulous** age. Even the great Joseph Banks took a keen and believing interest in a series of reported sightings of mermaids off the Scottish coast at the end of the eighteenth century.[75]

"There's no demand," said ... [a] gun dealer, busily sticking "Made in USA" labels on his stock of Brazilian pistols to impress **credulous** customers from across the Saudi border.[76]

write your own:

Daunt

'dȯnt or 'dänt

(Verb) to discourage (someone);
to threaten or intimidate
Keyword: haunt

Although people tried to discourage Timothy from entering the **haunted** house, he was brave and did not feel **daunted**.

After a near accident during her first drive, Annie realized what a **daunting** experience driving could be.

Metastatic breast cancer, severe emphysema, three operations, and several weeks in the hospital did not **daunt** her spirit.[79]

The threats are myriad. The challenges facing our country **daunting.**[80]

write your own:

Debacle

dE-'bä-k&l or de-b&-k&l

(Noun) a breakup; an overthrow; a sudden great disaster

Keyword: the buckle

Television stations were given hefty fines after televising the great Grammy **debacle** when a movie star showed up wearing only **the buckle**.

The fund raising car wash ended up being the biggest **debacle** in the school's history after two cars were stolen out of the parking lot.

Like a supercriminal, he can winch himself in and out of a filmic **debacle** before anyone knows....[83]

The service is slow, the drinks weak, and the food tastes like ripe garbage. You have two options during this painful experience. Option A: Critique the restaurant and smugly point out to your partner how wrong he or she was and how this **debacle** could have been avoided if only you had been listen to. Option B: Shut up and eat the food.[84]

write your own: _____

Deleterious

"de-l&-'ti-rE-&s

(Adjective) harmful or detrimental
Keyword: delete

With **deleterious** intent, the man **deleted** all the files on his company's computer after being fired.

It has been proven that smoking is **deleterious** to not only the smoker's health, but to those nearby who breathe in the smoke.

Likewise, there is no conclusive evidence linking **deleterious** human health effects to trace pesticide residues in the food supply.[87]

Although abstinence is obviously the safest course and is now advised by most doctors and public health officials, the fact is that we still do not know whether modest [a little] alcohol consumption has any **deleterious** effects on the fetus.[88]

write your own: _____

_____

Delineate

di-'li-nE-"At

(Verb) to indicate or describe/
to form the outer boundaries or outline of something
Keyword: deal on apes

The advertisement clearly **delineated** that the **deal on apes** would end at midnight.

The boundary of the basketball court is **delineated** by a thick black line.

This detailed artwork showcases the muscles used during each exercise and **delineates** how these muscles interact with surrounding joints and skeletal structures.[89]

What **delineates** the brilliant from the ordinary? Is it innovation or idiosyncrasy? Productivity or paradox?"[90]

write your own: _____

Section 2 Crossword Puzzle

Across

2. to indicate or describe/ to form the outer boundaries or outline of something
4. truthfulness or sincerity
6. attempting to unite or win over
7. a question or riddle that is difficult to solve
9. to discourage (someone); to threaten or intimidate
10. to punish or criticize harshly
13. a harsh assortment of loud and unpleasant sounds
14. cowardly; extreme defeatism
15. a person lacking manners or taste; a rude person
16. unpredictable, whimsical, or impulsive
17. using words that sound important in order to appear smarter

Down

1. distress or embarrassment caused by failure
3. to accept defeat unwillingly
4. gullible; too trusting
5. having knowledge of something; informed
8. harmful or detrimental
9. a breakup; an overthrow; a sudden great disaster
11. insubordinate, rebellious, or disobedient
12. to annul; cancel/ make a contrary order
15. to open up; to mention a subject

Section 2 Multiple Choice Review

Select the word that best fits each sentence.

1. Most of the employees considered the inconsiderate co-worker a _____ and tried to steer clear of him at all costs.
   a. debacle   b. conundrum   c. broach   d. boor

2. The students felt Susan sounded _____, as she enjoyed bragging about her job using the technical jargon she used at work.
   a. bombastic   b. cognizant   c. chagrin   d. composed

3. Much to my _____, the mall was not open when I got there.
   a. cacophony   b. chagrin   c. candor   d. conundrum

4. Walking into a new classroom in a new school, Michelle was not at all _____.
   a. deleterious   b. daunted   c. delineated   d. capitulated

5. As the tourists entered the jungle, they were greeted by a _____ of insect sounds.
   a. boor   b. cacophony   c. breach   d. candor

6. With surprising _____, the teacher stated he did not know the answer.
   a. cacophony   b. conciliation   c. debacle   d. candor

7. With Shannon's _____ tastes, her friends were never sure what to get her for her birthday.
   a. capricious   b. craven   c. bombastic   d. conciliatory

8. The _____ customer was banished from the store for her misbehavior.
   a. bombastic   b. contumacious   c. cognizant   d. credulous

9. An unsatisfied customer _____ the restaurant owner after discovering a dead fly in his soup.
   a. countermanded   b. delineated   c. daunted   d. castigated

10. Cindy was not sure how to _____ the subject of her bad grades with her parents.
    a. countermand   b. castigate   c. broach   d. capitulate

11. The president's advisor _____ after being harassed by the general public to resign from his position.
    a. countermanded   b. capitulated   c. delineated   d. daunted

12. A _____ plan was drawn up to stop further conflicts between the two fighting gangs.
    a. craven   b. conciliatory   c. bombastic   d. capricious

13. The opening night of the restaurant might not have been such a complete _____ if the owner had taken just a couple of extra months to prepare for the big event.
    a. boor   b. chagrin   c. broach   d. debacle

14. The logging industry has been very _____ to rain forests.
    a. deleterious   b. conundrum   c. capricious   d. bombastic

15. Middle East peace is a _____ that has been debated for decades.
    a. boor   b. cacophony   c. conundrum   d. countermand

16. The river clearly _____ the western boundary of the state.
    a. delineates   b. demurs   c. castigates   d. capitulates

17. Unsure of what play his opponent had in mind, Brian made a _____, but safe, move.
    a. craven   b. contumacious   c. chagrin   d. cognizant

18. Cecilia was extremely _____, believing that the mythical animals in the story really exist.
    a. candor   b. contumacious   c. credulous   d. craven

19. My father got upset with my mother when she _____ his discipline by allowing us to go to the party even when we were grounded.
    a. capitulated   b. broached   c. countermanded   d. delineated

20. It is often wondered, with all the people that receive traffic tickets, if they are _____ of all the traffic laws.
    a. credulous   b. cognizant   c. contumacious   d. craven

Section 2 Matching Review

Match the word on the left to the correct meaning on the right.

1. _____ Bombastic
2. _____ Boor
3. _____ Broach
4. _____ Cacophony
5. _____ Candor
6. _____ Capitulate
7. _____ Capricious
8. _____ Castigate
9. _____ Chagrin
10. _____ Cognizant
11. _____ Conciliatory
12. _____ Contumacious
13. _____ Conundrum
14. _____ Countermand
15. _____ Craven
16. _____ Credulous
17. _____ Daunt
18. _____ Debacle
19. _____ Deleterious
20. _____ Delineate

A. cowardly; extreme defeatism
B. attempting to unite or win over
C. gullible; too trusting
D. to indicate or describe/ to form the outer boundaries or outline of something
E. harmful or detrimental
F. to accept defeat unwillingly
G. a harsh assortment of loud and unpleasant sounds
H. a breakup; an overthrow; a sudden great disaster
I. to punish or criticize harshly
J. having knowledge of something; informed
K. unpredictable, whimsical, or impulsive
L. insubordinate, rebellious, or disobedient
M. using words that sound important in order to appear smarter
N. to discourage (someone); to threaten or intimidate
O. to open up; to mention a subject
P. to annul; cancel/ make a contrary order
Q. a question or riddle that is difficult to solve
R. distress or embarrassment caused by failure
S. truthfulness or sincerity
T. a person lacking manners or taste; a rude person

Section Three

Demagogue

'de-m&-"gäg

(Noun) a leader who usually appeals to people's emotions and prejudices

Keyword: denim dog

As a fashion **demagogue**, the **denim dog** influenced his fellow dogs to wear denim.

The leader of the cult was a **demagogue** who preyed on the emotions and prejudices of his group.

[He had to] quell his own revulsion at some of the lines he had to speak in those scenes where the fledgling Nazi **demagogue** starts addressing political meetings and discovers his capacity for rousing the rabble with hatred and invective.[91]

And the world is full of **demagogues** who have gotten away with advancing stupid or dangerous ideas because they've wrapped themselves in the cloak of religion.[92]

write your own:

Demur

di-'m&r

(Verb) to express hesitation or objection
Keyword: lemur

Because he ate the same thing day after day, the **lemur demurred** when given bananas again.

Tom **demurred** and argued with his mother after she insisted that he clean his room.

The Dutch have a word for people who are particularly stubborn, who keep going against all the odds. They're called kaaskops—cheeseheads—and John Langen doesn't **demur** when the label is put on him.[93]

Most players **demur** when asked about winning postseason awards, reciting, as if on automatic pilot, "If the team does well, that will take care of itself."[94]

write your own: _____

Denigration

"de-ni-'grA-sh&n"

(Noun) the act of making something seem not good or important
Keyword: demonstration

The audience showed increasing **denigration** for the magician's **demonstrations** because his tricks looked fake.

Sarah was put down and **denigrated** by others for having different political beliefs.

When you degrade, scold, or criticize yourself, you are out of alignment with the greater part of yourself, and there are no greater crippling thoughts than those of self-**denigration**.[91]

Columnist Andrew Bolt told the Victorian Supreme Court he didn't wage a campaign of **denigration** against [the] deputy chief magistrate [judge] ... but reported matters in the public interest when he criticized the court's "undue leniency [tolerance]."[92]

write your own:

Derision

di-'ri-zh&n

(Noun) ridicule or disrespect
Keyword: division

The student's inability to do **division** caused his classmates to treat him with **derision**.

Stuart faced **derision** at school because his classmates disapproved of his disruptive behavior.

As discussed throughout, verbal and physical **derision** or abuse in school should be considered a form of criminal behavior and punished accordingly. Peer cruelty is unacceptable and a clear violation of kids' rights.[95]

[He] did not want to be an object of **derision**; it was bad for discipline - and it was worse for discipline if the men shared some secret unknown to their officers.[96]

write your own: _____

Didactic

dI-'dak-tik

(Adjective) intended to be educational and informational/ aimed to teach a moral lesson

Keyword: died in the attic

A rat **died in the attic** as a result of listening to the long, boring, **didactic** lecture.

The church sponsored a **didactic** play designed to teach moral principles to the teenage audience.

It is history as it should be: entertaining without being glib [superficial], informative without being **didactic**.[103]

Organizers want that message—that we increase our awareness about the world around us and maybe even turn concern into action--to be delivered through a wide selection of films they say are not **didactic** or preachy but engaging and enlightening.[104]

write your own:

Diffidence

'di-f&-d&nts or 'di-f&-"dens

(Noun) unwillingness to speak or act because of low self confidence
Keyword: different dance

Because of her **diffidence** towards the tango, Holly waited for a **different dance** that she knew better.

After working out at the gym for several months, Jake became a more confident person, and his **diffidence** began to disappear.

His voice was icy now, full of command. All the trembling and **diffidence** gone.[103]

In fact, it was Howell's **diffidence**—an almost painful shyness in public and in private—that made him such a powerful antidote to Wilkins....[104]

write your own: _____

Dilatory

'di-l&-"tOr-E   or   'di-l&-"tor-E

(Adjective) causing delay or tending to procrastinate

Keyword: fill a story

Because she waited until the last minute to do her homework, the **dilatory** student decided to **fill a story** with many adjectives in order to meet the page requirement for the assignment.

His **dilatory** approach to his morning routine made him constantly late for work.

To quash a filibuster [a tactic to delay legislation] … Byrd arranged for then-Vice President Walter Mondale, the presiding officer of the Senate under the Constitution, to rule all **dilatory** amendments out of order.[107]

Sometimes the subject responds correctly but after a delay or in a **dilatory** manner. Often a sluggish response to commands is due to the fact that the subject has not been taught to respond quickly.[108]

write your own:

Discordant

'dis-"kor-d&nt

(Adjective) disagreeing; harsh sounding
Keyword: this cord

Pulling on the left cord chimes a pleasant sound. However, pulling on **this cord** will result in a loud **discordant** sound.

Though most reviews of the new restaurant were positive, there was one **discordant** review from a reporter who was displeased with the service.

Believe it or not, even very young babies notice whether music is harmonious or **discordant** and prefer harmonies.[109]

Better to go by the trees that sheltered the large colonies of fruit bats; the only assault there at that early hour was the bats' **discordant** concerts of squeaking and chattering.[110]

write your own:

Discursive

dis-'k&r-siv

(Adjective) changing topics
Keyword: curves

The teacher described a **discursive** essay as being a bad road with many **curves**, rambling in all directions.

In an attempt to steer the audience's questions away from the sensitive subject, the governor gave **discursive** answers to their inquiries.

While the movie's producers may have been trying to streamline Kerr's **discursive** collection of essays into a standard-issue Hollywood plotline, the result completely misses the point of Kerr's work....[107]

As such it has the **discursive** character of a diary, rather than the ordered structure of a more formally constructed piece.[108]

write your own:

Disparage

di-'spar-ij

(Verb) to criticize, degrade, or belittle
Keyword: the spare

Stuck in the middle of nowhere with a flat tire, he **disparaged** his friend for forgetting to replace **the spare**.

The governor's unpopular plan to raise taxes was **disparaged** in newspapers across the state.

I don't want to **disparage** mammography [procedure to detect breast cancer]; it is still the best detection tool we have right now. But by the time we can see a cancer, whether by mammography, ultrasound or MRI, it's often too far along.[113]

His rivalrous [given to conflict] anger is now directed away from the father, and towards himself. The boy is less prone to **disparage** the father, more prone to censure [criticize] himself....[114]

write your own: _____

Dogmatic

dog-'ma-tik

(Adjective) being certain that one is right; highly opinionated; authoritative

Keyword: dog mat

We should have warned the mailman that our dog Rufus is very **dogmatic** about who he will allow to step on his **dog mat**.

The religious organization was **dogmatic** and forceful in its beliefs.

Deeply spiritual, but never annoyingly **dogmatic**, she fixated on serving God in a professional capacity.[117]

They're very rigid and **dogmatic** about what the business needs to look like....[118]

write your own:

Dulcet

'd&l-s&t

(Adjective) pleasing to listen to; soothing
Keyword: dull set

Everyone thinks my grandma has a **dull set** of records. However, she considers the music **dulcet**, claiming it has a soothing and calming quality.

I couldn't decide which was more relaxing during my massage; the massage itself or the **dulcet** music playing in the background.

Peters's voice is one of the great instruments in the world of musical theatre—**dulcet** but full of attack, slightly mournful around the edges.[119]

They manage to argue in **dulcet** tones for the remainder of the meal while Sima and I exchanged wan [gloomy] smiles across the table.[120]

write your own:

Duplicity

du-'pli-s&-tE or dyu-'pli-s&-tE

(Noun) deception, dishonesty, or double-dealing

Keyword: Duplex City

In his **duplicity**, the realtor tricked the two families into buying the same home in **Duplex City**.

The double agent went to prison after his **duplicity** in spying was discovered.

There was an element of **duplicity** in Wilson's dealings here.[121]

Perhaps the greatest contradiction in [Mr.] Pound is that as clearly as he sees the **duplicity** and corruption in the so-called movement, he still trusts in it.[122]

write your own:

Eclectic

e-'klek-tik or i-'klek-tik

(Adjective) selecting or choosing from various sources
Keyword: electric

Johnny powered his **electric** car using several **eclectic** energy sources including solar, nuclear, wind, and battery.

Raymond was baffled by her **eclectic** taste in music. She liked rock 'n roll, country, punk, reggae, and polka.

The four grand streets of Burns, Iroquois, Seminole, and Adams were lined with stately houses built in **eclectic** styles. Red-brick Georgian rose next to English Tudor, which gave onto French provincial.[121]

In fact, what the skyscrapers at the end of Manhattan represented is an immensely complex and **eclectic** civilization. New York City is the most cosmopolitan place in the history of the world....[122]

write your own: _____

Efficacious

"e-f&-'kA-sh&s

(Adjective) effective; capable of producing the desired effect
Keyword: effective cages

His search for **effective cages** proved **efficacious** when he discovered a model with a new lock that even Houdini could not escape from.

The seat belt is an **efficacious** safety device that reduces the number of personal injuries in accidents.

Both Beaton's Guide and my own dim memories of folk medicine held that [a] spider's web was **efficacious** in dressing wounds.[123]

So the Prime Minister rose to his feet in the House of Commons on March 18th and gave the least tender and most **efficacious** speech of his career.[124]

write your own:

Effluvia

e-'flü-vE-&

(Noun) a toxic odor or vapor
Note: Effluvium is singular
Keyword: flu

The **effluvia** from the science lab resulted in a **flu** epidemic at school.

Specialists were brought into the home that was suspected to have noxious leaks of **effluvia** circulating in the air.

This is the time of year when many of us survey the maze of critics' "top 10" lists and respond, in the mode of John McEnroe, "You can't be serious." How could anyone conjure up such a mixed bag of cinematic [related to motion pictures] **effluvia**?[127]

Soviet industrial projects account for many of the detonations [explosions], which, along with [nuclear] reactor **effluvia**, have deposited most of the world's nuclear waste in the region, including at least six reactors dumped off the coast.[128]

write your own:

Effrontery

i-'fr&n-t&-rE or e-'fr&n-t&-rE

(Noun) boldness, nerve, or courage
Keyword: in front of me

As the king gave Arthur a medal of honor he said, "This man showed great **effrontery** by standing **in front of me** during the battle."

With **effrontery**, the student spoke in his graduation speech about changes that needed to be made to the school administration.

Book Title: Samuel Johnson's Book of Insults: A Compendium of Snubs, Sneers, Slights and **Effronteries** from the 18th Century's Master.[129]

Just between ourselves, I continually wonder at my own **effrontery** in opposing this young man who's going to do so much for us all.[130]

write your own:

Embroil

im-'broi&l or im-'broil

(Verb) to involve in confusion or conflict
Keyword: boil

The chefs became **embroiled** in a dispute over whether to **boil** or broil the fish.

The reluctance of the factory to clean up the sewage could **embroil** them in a lawsuit with the local community.

Her father is determined not to **embroil** his family in a messy, high-profile murder case.[127]

Every true friend to this Country must see and feel that the policy of it is not to **embroil** ourselves with any nation whatsoever; but to avoid their disputes and politics; and if they will harass one another, to avail ourselves of the neutral conduct we have adopted. - President George Washington[128]

write your own: _____

http://SolidA.net ©Solid A, Inc. 87

Empirical

im-'pir-i-k&l

(Adjective) based on what is experienced or observed
Keyword: empire

The billionaire's **empire** was built on **empirical** data of experience and observations of the stock market.

The students learned how to record **empirical** data they gathered in science class.

Art is not the best medium for representing **empirical** data, as the artist, by definition, has a big hand in any outcome.[133]

But all this is speculation. Nobody has a shred of **empirical** evidence that any of these influences actually boost IQ (Intelligence Quotient).[134]

write your own:

Encumber

in-'k&m-b&r

(Verb) to hinder; restrict motion/ burden
Keyword: cucumber

Carrying the **cucumber encumbered** the man so much, he was unable to walk with it very far.

Thanks to luggage wheels, fewer people are **encumbered** by the heavy baggage they take with them while traversing through airports.

By looking at boys in a narrow way and failing to recognize the gentle, creative, empathic sides of many boys, I believe that some teachers—though they may not consciously intend it—can seriously **encumber** the emotional and scholastic development of boys in their classes....[129]

She cuts through the clutter of details that **encumber** many conversations and focuses on the heart of the matter.[130]

write your own: _____

Section 3 Crossword Puzzle

Across

2. to express hesitation or objection
4. being certain that one is right; highly opinionated; authoritative
6. changing topics
9. ridicule or disrespect
10. effective; capable of producing the desired effect
11. to involve in confusion or conflict
13. a leader who usually appeals to people's emotions and prejudices
15. pleasing to listen to; soothing
17. selecting or choosing from various sources

Down

1. the act of making something seem not good or important
2. intended to be educational and informational
3. to criticize, to degrade, or belittle
5. to hinder; restrict motion/ burden
7. based on what is experienced or observed
8. disagreeing; harsh sounding
9. unwillingness to speak or act because of low selfconfidence
12. causing delay or tending to procrastinate
14. boldness, nerve, or courage
15. deception, dishonesty, or double-dealing
16. a toxic odor or vapor

Section 3 Multiple Choice Review

Select the word that best fits each sentence.

1. Part of what made the hypnotist so powerful was his _____ voice that lulled people into a deep sleep.
   a. didactic   b. discursive   c. dulcet   d. empirical

2. Josh finally decided to quit his job because he could no longer take the constant _____ from his co-workers.
   a. dogma   b. demagogue   c. denigration   d. duplicity

3. After extensive testing, the drug proved to be _____ and was soon released into the drug market.
   a. efficacious   b. encumbered   c. empirical   d. eclectic

4. The waiter was so angered by the _____ of his customer, that he switched tables with his co-worker.
   a. effrontery   b. diffidence   c. discordance   d. demur

5. Because of his _____ when dealing with others, Robert lost two of his closest friends when they discovered he lied to them.
   a. effluvia   b. denigration   c. effrontery   d. duplicity

6. To let the management know they did not like the new employment policies, the employees shouted hoots of _____ after it was read.
   a. derision   b. denigration   c. effluvia   d. demur

7. The _____ data was/were not entirely reliable. More research would be required before the product could be made available to the public.
   a. dulcet   b. eclectic   c. empirical   d. dilatory

8. While classes were closed, teachers attended a workshop designed to change the way they taught from a traditional _____ approach to a more discovery-based approach.
   a. didactic   b. discursive   c. embroiled   d. disparaging

9. Maggie's _____ at the meeting led people to believe that she was stuck up, when in reality she was very timid.
   a. derision   b. diffidence   c. duplicity   d. effluvia

10. Chris refused to get _____ with his best friend's fights.
    a. embroiled   b. disparaged   c. dogmatic   d. didactic

11. The overloaded truck had a(n) _____ effect on the flow of traffic, causing the traffic to back up for miles.
    a. discordant   b. dilatory   c. eclectic   d. empirical

12. The weight of the problems of the city _____ the mayor and visibly aged him while he held the office.
    a. encumbered   b. embroiled   c. disparaged   d. demurred

13. The international students served an _____ cuisine from four continents at the banquet.
    a. embroiled   b. encumbered   c. eclectic   d. efficacious

14. The girl's _____ insistence that Zaire was located in Central America proved to be wrong.
    a. discursive   b. encumbered   c. dogmatic   d. dulcet

15. Students were warned to be cautious of _____ while conducting science experiments.
    a. duplicity   b. effluvia   c. derision   d. effrontery

16. Though the student was eager to partake in the English composition class, his first paper received a bad grade due to its incoherent thesis statement and its _____ organization.
    a. discursive   b. didactic   c. empirical   d. dilatory

17. When the opposing team showed up in the stadium, _____ booing exploded from the crowd.
    a. diffident   b. discursive   c. didactic   d. discordant

18. The brilliant _____ rocketed his way to political prominence by appealing to the emotions and prejudices of the people.
    a. effluvia   b. demagogue   c. dogma   d. denigration

19. Even though she was required to take a foreign language at school, Lacey _____ because she had never been very good with learning new languages.
    a. encumbered   b. denigrated   c. disparaged   d. demurred

20. After the company went bankrupt, both the workers and the public immediately _____ the CEO and the president with a harsh article about their incompetence in the newspaper.
    a. disparaged   b. demurred   c. encumbered   d. embroiled

Section 3 Matching Review

Match the word on the left to the correct meaning on the right.

1. _____ Demagogue
2. _____ Demur
3. _____ Denigration
4. _____ Derision
5. _____ Didactic
6. _____ Diffidence
7. _____ Dilatory
8. _____ Discordant
9. _____ Discursive
10. _____ Disparage
11. _____ Dogmatic
12. _____ Dulcet
13. _____ Duplicity
14. _____ Eclectic
15. _____ Efficacious
16. _____ Effluvia
17. _____ Effrontery
18. _____ Embroil
19. _____ Empirical
20. _____ Encumber

A. deception, dishonesty, or double-dealing
B. ridicule or disrespect
C. a leader who usually appeals to people's emotions and prejudices
D. to criticize, degrade, or belittle
E. selecting or choosing from various sources
F. a toxic odor or vapor
G. changing topics
H. being certain that one is right; highly opinionated; authoritative
I. based on what is experienced or observed
J. causing delay or tending to procrastinate
K. boldness, nerve, or courage
L. unwillingness to speak or act because of low self confidence
M. to hinder; restrict motion/burden
N. effective; capable of producing the desired effect
O. to express hesitation or objection
P. to involve in confusion or conflict
Q. pleasing to listen to; soothing
R. disagreeing; harsh sounding
S. intended to be educational and informational
T. the act of making something seem not good or important

Section Four

Enervate

'e-n&r-"vAt

(Verb) to weaken or unnerve;
to reduce the mental or moral vigor
Keyword: nerve

Caution: enervate is nearly the opposite of energy

After spending twenty-four continuous hours removing a tumor from the patient's entangled **nerves**, the surgeon felt **enervated** and wiped out.

The well conditioned basketball team's strategy was to continue to increase the tempo on both ends of the court in order to **enervate** the opposing team.

Huntington created a hierarchy of civilizations based upon climactic advantage or disadvantage: cool climates stimulate civilizational energies, while tropical climates **enervate**.[131]

[Barry Bonds yelled] "Man, I'm burned out!" And that was before the Giants played the kind of white-knuckle marathon against the Diamondbacks that **enervates** the winners as much as the losers.[132]

write your own:

Enigma

i-'nig-m& or e-'nig-m&

(Noun) a puzzling riddle; something unexplainable
Keyword: In a wig ma?

"Is that you **in a wig, ma**?" It was a real **enigma** when ma started wearing an oversized wig.

Even after hours of explanation, the math problem remained an **enigma** to the class.

Domestic cats harbor their own mysteries, of course, but sometimes the **enigma** lies more within owner than pet.[135]

Early in his rehabilitation, Lathrop couldn't keep from reflecting on the **enigma** that has plagued and inspired so many artists and philosophers throughout the history of Western art and thought—the question of human suffering under a supposedly benevolent God.[136]

write your own: _____

Ephemeral

i-'fem-r&l or i-'fEm-r&l

(Adjective) fleeting, short lived, or transitory

Keyword: emeralds

Susan's engagement was **ephemeral** after discovering that her **emerald** ring was made of plastic.

The song had **ephemeral** success on the radio, and was taken off the air shortly after its debut since it offended many people.

A close [completion of a business agreement] that you get by following Technique 14 is likely to be both artificial and **ephemeral**. Because it's built on trickery, it can never bring you the sustained business that every professional wants.[137]

All human life is likened to evening dew and morning frost, considered something quite fragile and **ephemeral**.[138]

write your own:

Epitome

i-'pi-t&-mE

(Noun) a part that represents the whole/ perfect example of something/ summary
Keyword: pits for me

Out of all of my workers, John is the **epitome** of an ideal construction worker, digging hundreds of **pits for me**.

The training session was the **epitome** of what the job would be like, and helped him determine if he would like the job.

Breuer was the **epitome** of the family doctor; he made house calls and would see patients as early as 6:30 a.m.[139]

In the United States, models and actresses are held up as the **epitome** of beauty, yet these women who grace the covers of magazines and star in films know that their careers would be cut short if they didn't protect their most precious asset— their skin.[140]

write your own: _____

Equivocal

i-'kwi-v&-k&l

(Adjective) subject to multiple interpretations; questionable; ambiguous

Keyword: quiver

As the judge's ruling was **equivocal**, the convict imagined the worst and began to **quiver**, not understanding the ambiguous nature of his sentence.

The detective's responses were purposely **equivocal** so the public would remain unaware until an official report was released.

Evidence for true cannibalism among dinosaurs is **equivocal**. ... Analyses of chewed bones suggest that tyrannosaurs often ate tyrannosaurs, but the teeth marks aren't distinctive enough to determine whether victim and predator were members of the same species.[141]

Nothing is more **equivocal**. There are guilty men who can hide a true crime ... and innocent victims who confess to crimes of which they were not guilty.[142]

write your own:

Erudite

'er-&-"dIt or 'er-y&-"dIt

(Adjective) learned; scholarly
Keyword: air tight

After years of research, the **erudite** scientists discovered a new **air tight** storage system that kept his hamburger fresh for months.

The **erudite** professional organization had strict criteria to ensure that all of its prospective members were well read, intelligent, and had earned recognition in their chosen field of study.

Some of us also have an inferiority complex about poetry, viewing it as an art that only the well-educated, literate, and **erudite** can appreciate.[139]

As the Astro's resident intellectual, Brad Ausmus isn't known for his tirades. He is, by nature, soft-spoken and thoughtful to the point of being **erudite**.[140]

write your own:

Esoteric

"e-s&-'ter-ik or "e-s&-'te-rik
(Adjective) understood by very few people/
strange or unusual
Keyword: S.O.S.

On the video, the prisoner of war used his eyes to blink an **esoteric S.O.S.** while being forced to make a false statement that he was being treated well.

Her strange and **esoteric** taste in clothes was appreciated by very few people who knew her.

Consider this description of the job from a critic at a midsize daily: "Unlike movie critics or drama critics, [art critics] regularly deal with **esoteric** and obscure art forms that the average newspaper reader might find baffling."[143]

Bruce Thompson holds one of Maryland government's more **esoteric** jobs—assistant state underwater archaeologist....[144]

write your own:

Evanescent

"e-v&-'ne-s&nt

(Adjective) fade away; disappear; vanish
Keyword: heaven sent

Heaven sent an angel to tell me something, but the **evanescent** vision disappeared too quickly.

Great ideas are often **evanescent**. Before you have a chance to write them down, you have already forgotten them.

What is athletic greatness if it doesn't have contagious properties? Only as **evanescent** as the smoke of a fine cigar.[143]

And so film [is] by nature the most transparent and **evanescent** of art forms, the one best suited to revealing the motion of our lives....[144]

write your own:

Evince

i-'vints or i-'vins

(Verb) to show or manifest in an obvious way. to display clearly; reveal
Keyword: evidence

The **evidence evinced** to everyone that John was responsible for tracking in the mud.

It was strange to learn that Traci enjoys canoeing so much as she has always **evinced** a fear of water.

"Do you have any questions for me?" There was a long silence, and the head of the school was acutely uncomfortable, fearing that no boy would **evince** any interest at all and the school would be embarrassed.[147]

"The canoes," [Meriwether] Louis wrote on February 22, "along with the woodwork and sculpture of these people (Native Americans) as well as these hats and their waterproof baskets **evince** ingenuity common among the Aborigines of America."[148]

write your own:

Exacerbate

ig-'za-s&r-"bAt

(Verb) to aggravate; to make worse
Keyword: exact bait

Caution: Not to be confused with exasperate or exaggerate

The storeowner **exacerbated** the already angry customers by providing them with **exact bait** by measuring each worm with a ruler.

The current agricultural problems were further **exacerbated** by the drought.

Pataki has vowed to veto the State Legislature's aid package, saying it would **exacerbate** the state's budget deficit.[145]

Anxiety is now believed to **exacerbate** diabetes by raising levels of the stress hormone cortisol, which regulates insulin and blood-sugar levels.[146]

write your own:

Exculpate

'ek-sk&l-"pAt

(Verb) to clear from a charge of guilt or fault

Keyword: X skull

The pirate was **exculpated** and released after it was discovered that he was not responsible for vandalizing the ship with the "**X skull**" spray painting.

The defendant was **exculpated** of all charges after the real culprit was discovered.

Should you draw the death penalty in this state, you have thirty days to find any evidence that would **exculpate** you.[149]

Leppo quickly moved to have the charges thrown out on the basis of the detective's contradictory testimony and on the grounds that the lost evidence might help **exculpate** his client.[150]

write your own:

Exhortation

"ek-"sor-'tA-sh&n or eg-"z&r-'tA-h&n

(Noun) encouragement; to move one to action by argument, advice, or request
Keyword: egg sort station

After dozens of bad eggs were returned to their store, the **exhortation** of the salesman to buy an **egg sort station** was quickly approved.

The magazine article included an **exhortation** encouraging consumers to recycle their newspapers.

His drawn brows and the deep furrow between them showed that he needed no **exhortation** to concentrate all his attention upon a problem....[147]

As she herself acknowledged, she found it impossible to write a short letter, and to John Quincy and Charles came pages dispensing vigorous, motherly **exhortations**. "Strive to excel," she urged Charles. "Anything worth doing was worth doing well, she reminded them."[148]

write your own: _____

Exonerate

ig-'zä-n&-"rAt or eg-'zä-n&-"rAt

(Verb) to clear of guilt or blame
Keyword: eggs on her plate

After the food fight Jen was **exonerated** because she still had all of her **eggs on her plate**, proving she did not take part in the fight.

The owner's ex-wife was **exonerated** of all suspicion after it was revealed the house fire was caused by an electrical failure.

A disturbing number of the veterans of Watergate seemed only too willing to **exonerate** Clinton for conduct that eerily resembled Nixon's....[149]

He kept a private diary! Yes, a diary, in which he placed all the blame on his wife! He was determined to make sure that coming generations would **exonerate** him and put the blame on his wife.[150]

write your own:

Extenuating/Extenuate

ik-'sten-y&-"wAt-ng

(Verb) to lessen the seriousness; make less blameworthy; excusing

*Extenuating is a verb that functions as an adjective

Keyword: exterminating

Due to **extenuating** circumstances, **exterminating** the bugs was put to a quick stop after it was discovered that the bugs were endangered.

Rick did not care about any **extenuating** conditions that surrounded the car accident; he was going to be mad regardless as a result of the damage to his car.

No matter how **extenuating** the circumstances, no one else gets the blame if the plows are too slow. Snow removal can make or break a political career.[153]

Assuredly, Madame, you are determined to **extenuate** certain things and exaggerate others.[154]

write your own:

Extricate

'ek-str&-"kAt

Verb) to remove or free (someone or something); to set free
Keyword: extra cage

Due to the large number of rabbits born in the spring, the zoo keeper **extricated** the rabbits from the **extra cages** by releasing them in the countryside.

It took the tow truck several hours to **extricate** the van from the snow bank.

He managed to **extricate** himself, and then fell into another, deeper, crevasse.[153]

How do we **extricate** our emotions, mind, body, and spirit from the agony of entanglement?[154]

write your own:

Fabricate

'fa-bri-"kAt

(Verb) to make up a story
Keyword: fabric

In order to increase the sales at the **fabric** store, Gail **fabricated** a story about how the fabric was woven by hand by women in a remote indigenous tribe.

Greg knew that he had to **fabricate** a good story to tell his parents about the tragic condition of the house, or else they would never leave him home alone for a weekend again.

When I had told everything I could safely **fabricate** [the interrogators] asked no more questions.[155]

When she proudly refused to let him **fabricate** a scandal about her, he had her blacklisted.[156]

write your own:

Fallacious

f&-'lA-sh&s

(Adjective) misleading; tending to deceive
Keyword: fillet of fish

The packaging on the **fillet of fish** was **fallacious** because it was actually thinly sliced chicken.

Though Kristin's speech was good, her research and reasoning were based on **fallacious** findings.

In the first few days of the war, both newspapers slanted their headlines in an attempt to bolster their **fallacious** predictions.... The situation was so egregious [conspicuously bad] that I actually got mad at the pulp fiction that was in my hands.[157]

To survive these ordeals the new idea must be correct, as the **fallacious** and unsound ones are destroyed by the attacks made upon them.[158]

write your own:

Fastidious

fa-'sti-dE-&s or f&-'sti-dE-&s

(Adjective) hard to please/ meticulous with details
Keyword: fast idiots

Not pleased with the selection of beverages offered at the drink station in the marathon, the **fast idiots** were extremely **fastidious** and refused to drink anything.

The **fastidious** guests did not like anything the hostess was serving.

In the past, the Times editorial page had been criticized for being ... too **fastidious**.[159]

Industry insiders say Williams, Aetna's chief of health operations, is **fastidious**, a nut for detail....[160]

write your own: _____

Fatuous

'fa-chü-&s or 'fa-tyü-&s

(Adjective) stupid; lacking good sense; foolish or silly

Keyword: fat

The **fat** hog was known for upsetting the other farm animals with his **fatuous** remarks.

Her **fatuous** suggestions about how the reception should be run was unbelievably stupid and in bad taste.

A lot of the trendy stuff is really just **fatuous** nonsense....[159]

The Kenyans are to distance running what the Yankees once were to baseball: so infuriatingly good that even aspiring to beat them seems to be an act of **fatuous** optimism.[160]

write your own:

Feckless

'fek-l&s

(Adjective) ineffective/ without care or responsibility
Keyword: freckles

John never bothered to use sunscreen. As a result of this **feckless** attitude, he ended up with lots of **freckles**.

Because Darlene was a **feckless** rider, she got bucked off of the horse.

Nelson personifies **feckless** slackerdom.[161]

Didn't dirty water come from the neglect of **feckless**, greedy governments?[162]

write your own:

Section 4 Crossword Puzzle

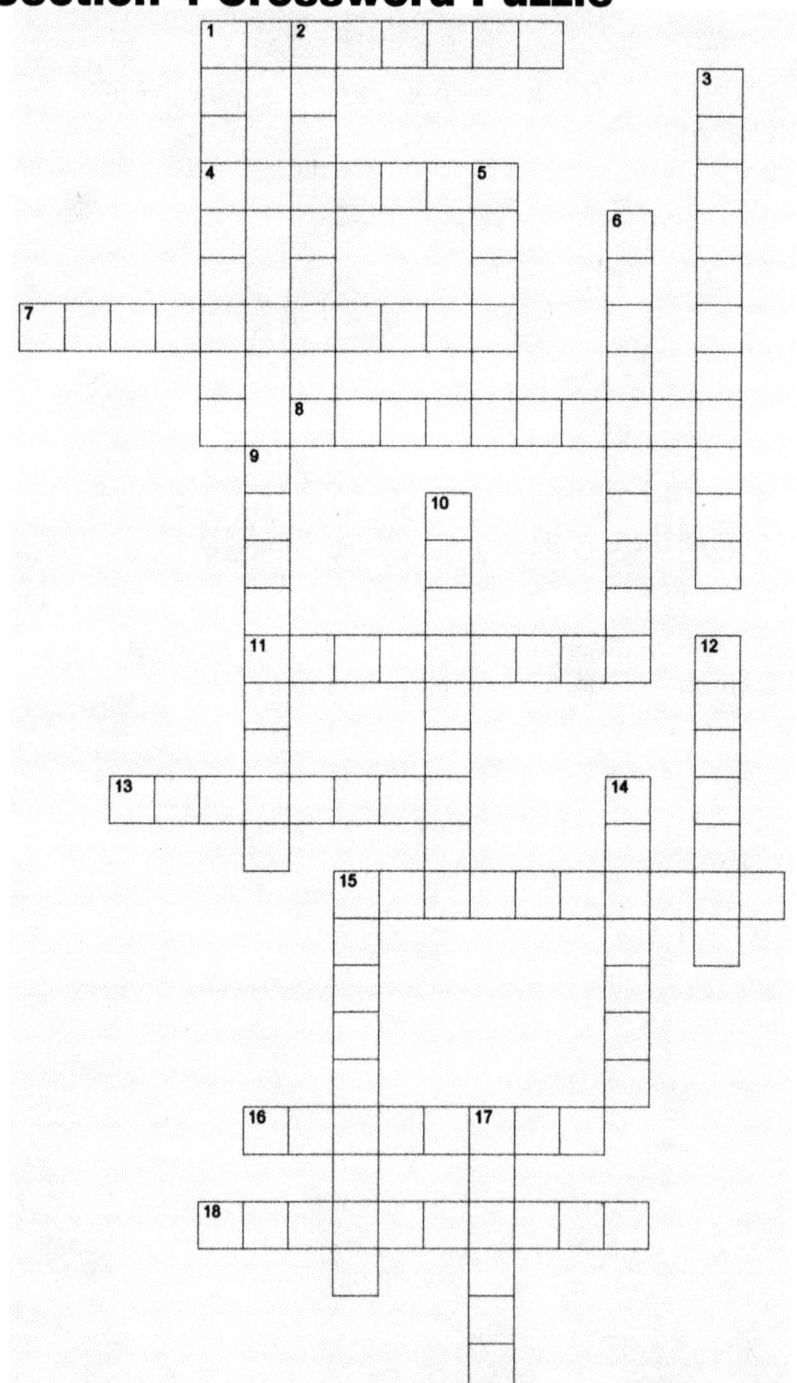

Across

1. to weaken or unnerve; to reduce the mental or moral vigor
4. learned; scholarly
7. encouragement; to move one to action by argument, advice, or request
8. fade away; disappear; vanish
11. to remove or free (someone or something); to set free
13. understood by very few people/ strange or unusual
15. misleading; tending to deceive
16. ineffective/ without care or responsibility
18. hard to please/ meticulous with details

Down

1. fleeting, short live, or transitory
2. to clear from a charge of guilt or fault
3. to lessen the seriousness; make less blameworthy; excusing
5. to show or manifest in an obvious way
6. to aggravate; to make worse
9. to clear of guilt or blame
10. subject to multiple interpretations; questionable; ambiguous
12. stupid; lacking good sense
14. a part that represents the whole/ perfect example of something/ summary
15. to make up a story
17. a puzzling riddle; something unexplainable

Section 4 Multiple Choice Review

Select the word that best fits each sentence.

1. Joseph's bad day on Friday was the _____ of his whole week.
   a. ephemeral   b. exhortation   c. esoteric   d. epitome

2. The poor report card _____ the problems she was already having with her mother.
   a. enervated   b. fabricated   c. exacerbated   d. exonerated

3. The _____ director was picky in his attention to detail for the movie.
   a. fastidious   b. erudite   c. fallacious   d. feckless

4. The student was _____ from cheating on the exam, after he proved he worked out the problems himself.
   a. exculpated   b. exonerated   c. enervated   d. extricated

5. It was rather a(n) _____ why she broke up with him.
   a. epitome   b. enigma   c. erudite   d. erudite

6. The entire report regarding the condition of the store was _____, including the names of the owners.
   a. fallacious   b. fastidious   c. evinced   d. feckless

7. Kenny, the _____ professor, specialized in women's literature and Shakespeare at the university.
   a. fallacious   b. fatuous   c. fastidious   d. erudite

8. The teacher was frustrated when she called on a student, who was obviously not paying attention. His _____ answer made the whole class laugh.
   a. equivocal   b. evanescent   c. fatuous   d. ephemeral

9. Lila left out any _____ circumstances when describing the evening to her mother so that she would not get into trouble.
   a. fatuous   b. equivocal   c. extenuating   d. exonerating

10. The children's excitement about swimming was _____ because it started to rain just after they left for the pool.
    a. ephemeral   b. evinced   c. fatuous   d. feckless

11. No one completely understood the movie star's many _____ statements on the TV talk show.
    a. evanescent   b. fallacious   c. equivocal   d. fabricated

12. Unable to appreciate or understand their brother's strange fetish for cereal boxes, Lance's collection remained _____.
    a. fatuous   b. esoteric   c. extraneous   d. ephemeral

13. Because his students _____ a love for the outdoors, the teacher held class outside.
    a. fabricated   b. evinced   c. extenuated   d. extricated

14. The child was _____ when his older brother stepped forward and admitted guilt to the broken mirror.
    a. exacerbated   b. evinced   c. extenuated   d. exculpated

15. The oasis was a(n) _____ vision, disappearing as soon as the wanderer reached the pool.
    a. fallacious   b. evanescent   c. feckless   d. fastidious

16. Despite the _____ of the owners to play somewhere else, the neighborhood kids continued to loiter outside of the convenience store.
    a. exhortation   b. enigma   c. exoneration   d. epitome

17. In an attempt to _____ the kite from the tree, Jeff ended up tearing the kite.
    a. enervate   b. exhonerate   c. extricate   d. exculpate

18. Though Joan sat down to do her homework, her _____ and lackadaisical approach left her unable to complete the assignment on time.
    a. feckless   b. exhortation   c. equivocal   d. esoteric

19. The hot, humid air and the hard physical work _____ the teenagers so much they wanted to take a nap.
    a. exacerbated   b. exculpated   c. enervated   d. extricated

20. Though everyone knew they were _____, we all enjoyed listening to Bill's stories about what he did over the weekend.
    a. evanescent   b. erudite   c. esoteric   d. fabricated

Section 4 Matching Review

Match the word on the left to the correct meaning on the right.

1. _____ Enervate
2. _____ Enigma
3. _____ Ephemeral
4. _____ Epitome
5. _____ Equivocal
6. _____ Erudite
7. _____ Esoteric
8. _____ Evanescent
9. _____ Evince
10. _____ Exacerbate
11. _____ Exculpate
12. _____ Exhortation
13. _____ Exonerate
14. _____ Extenuating
15. _____ Extricate
16. _____ Fabricate
17. _____ Fallacious
18. _____ Fastidious
19. _____ Fatuous
20. _____ Feckless

A. a puzzling riddle; something unexplainable
B. learned; scholarly
C. to clear of guilt or blame
D. to aggravate; to make worse
E. misleading; tending to deceive
F. to make up a story
G. fleeting, short live, or transitory
H. encouragement; to move one to action by argument, advice, or request
I. to show or manifest in an obvious way
J. ineffective/ without care or responsibility
K. fade away; disappear; vanish
L. to lessen the seriousness; make less blameworthy; excusing
M. subject to multiple interpretations; questionable; ambiguous
N. to clear from a <u>charge</u> of guilt or fault
O. to remove or free (someone or something); to set free
P. hard to please/ meticulous with details
Q. a part that represents the whole/ perfect example of something/ summary
R. stupid; lacking good sense
S. understood by very few people/ strange or unusual
T. to weaken or unnerve; to reduce the mental or moral vigor

Section Five

Florid

'flor-&d or 'flär-&d

(Adjective) having too much decoration; gaudy/ flushed; tinged with red

Keyword: floral

The **floral** hat, decorated with gaudy looking flowers, was far too **florid** to wear to the party.

The interior designer had a habit of over-decorating and consequently became well known for the **florid** rooms she created.

The little man tugged an enormous suitcase out onto the porch, never taking notice of me, his **florid** face streaked with perspiration.[163]

In a minute, a short man with a **florid** face and bald head came out of the office with quick, hurried steps, like a mouse running from a hole in the wall.[164]

write your own:

Flout

'flaut

(Verb) to disregard or disobey intentionally
Keyword: trout

The **trout flouted** the sign and decided to swim wherever he wished.

At the end of the last day of school, the group of rowdy students decided to **flout** the school rules and race down the hall, making as much noise as possible.

The independent television commission said that if YOU TV continued to **flout** its codes of practice, it would consider taking the channel off air.[165]

From a Yankee perspective, these laws may seem unjust. But is that sufficient reason to **flout** them?[166]

write your own:

Foment

'fO-"ment or fO-'ment
(Verb) to stir up or arouse
Keyword: foam

When the hottest teenage icon appeared wearing a **foam** outfit, a new fashion trend was **fomented** among teenagers.

The students were seated across the room from each other because they were sure to **foment** disturbances if they were together.

He knows how critical the fans in Philadelphia can be, how sports radio there can **foment** controversy...[169]

The powers in London, worried that Oglethorpe would **foment** war with Spain with his colonization and fortifications, asked him to withdraw from the coastal islands.[170]

write your own:

Frenetic

fri-'ne-tik

(Adjective) frantic, wildly excited, or uncontrolled
Keyword: friend's attic

He became **frenetic** after finding a rare baseball card in his **friend's attic**.

George was looking forward to retirement when he could put his **frenetic** life-style behind and just relax for a while.

[She] has been a harsh critic of children's programming—Mister Rogers excepted. Typically, she says, the **frenetic** pacing, adult irony and consumerist agenda is, at the very least, inappropriate.[169]

Anne Arundel County's new planning chief, whose **frenetic** work schedule has earned him the moniker [nickname] "Ironman," is rebuilding the county's planning office....[170]

write your own:

Fulsome

'ful-s&m

(Adjective) praise too positive to be considered sincere or genuine/ abundant; generous in amount

Keyword: full slum

Tremendously thankful for a place to sleep, the homeless man gave the **full slum** an extremely high **fulsome** rating.

The realtor's **fulsome** praise for the house was a little too unrealistic, and therefore we decided not to buy the home.

[President Franklin Delano Roosevelt's] typical campaign speech, the York Herald Tribune said, began with "a few words of **fulsome** praise for Alfred E. Smith."[171]

[He] was **fulsome** in his praise of Tim Byrne yesterday, saying his chief executive had done "an amazing job" and had his "total confidence."[172]

write your own:

Furtive

'f&r-tiv

(Adjective) done secretly so as not to be noticed by others
Keyword: fur live

The bear skin rug pretended to be dead during the day, but the **fur lived** at night by **furtively** eating leftovers.

Cindy suspected Peter had a secret crush on her after she caught him repeatedly casting **furtive** glances at her.

There was nothing **furtive** about the protest that took place in bright sunshine surrounding Cherry Cheek Shopping Center Friday. At least seven animal-rights groups ... joined forces, placards [posters] and passion in protesting swanky [fashionably elegant] shopping icon Neiman Marcus for selling furs.[173]

Most of his (characters) spend some of their time snatching **furtive** glimpses of people from behind their curtains ....[174]

write your own:

Garrulous

'gar-&-l&s or 'gar-y&-l&s

(Adjective) talkative, usually about unimportant things
Keyword: gargle

Garrulous Gus can't stop talking, even when he **gargles**.

At home Frank is laconic, but at work he is **garrulous**—rarely pausing for a second between words.

I'm pretty sure from his description that this inside man was the same guy I and a dozen other journalists interviewed.... It is unlikely that there was more than one **garrulous** Canadian advising the Haitian junta and talking to reporters.[179]

In the movies, your typical gangster is a fast-talking joker, a wise-crack machine brimming with raunchy, unprintable quips [clever remark]. In real life, though, mobsters tend to be a bit less **garrulous**.[180]

write your own:

Gratuitous

gr&-'tü-&-t&s or gr&-'tyü-&-t&s

(Adjective) not required; uncalled for/ free or voluntary

Keyword: gut stew for us

On our exotic honeymoon our chef added a **gratuitous** bowl of **gut stew for us**, a local delicacy, which we had not ordered.

The film depicted **gratuitous** violence that was unnatural and forced into the script.

The empty shells of heavy [weaponry] lay everywhere, as did the twisted wrecks of cars, trucks, tanks, and APCs. The impression of vast, **gratuitous** destruction and carnage was only underlined and framed by the weirdly ordinary.[181]

His warts-and-all portraits include a few perhaps **gratuitous** details....[182]

write your own: _____

Gregarious

gri-'gar-E-&s or gri-'ger-E-&s

(Adjective) enjoying the company of others; outgoing or social

Keyword: hilarious

The **gregarious** young boy was always surrounded by friends because he was so outgoing and **hilarious**.

Kelsey's **gregarious** personality made her a great candidate for living in a sorority.

When hired, **gregarious** blackjack dealers and roulette spinners give new meaning to having a game face: They wish gamblers luck, directing them to machines and tables that have produced winners. When customers hit the jackpot, there are high-fives and kudos.[179]

He doesn't smile a lot; he's not especially warm or **gregarious**; his dress is subdued and professional. Even his manner of speaking is quiet, monotone, often stern and blunt.[180]

write your own:

Guile

'gI&l or 'gIl

(Noun) trickery or deceit
Keyword: pile

The con artist used a lot of trickery and **guile** to produce a **pile** of loot.

Starving from hunger and malnutrition, the villagers relied on **guile** to swindle money and goods from the unsuspecting tourists.

Smith, 37, used his experience and **guile** to exploit the weaknesses of Buffalo's young receiver, Peerless Price, on a day when Bill's quarterback Drew Bledsoe threw 51 passes.[183]

Integrity also means avoiding any communication that is deceptive, full of **guile**, or beneath the dignity of people.[184]

write your own:

Hapless

'ha-pl&s

(Adjective) unlucky or unfortunate
Keyword: hatless

The **hapless** hat salesman became **hatless** after a strong wind blew all of his hats out to sea.

The **hapless** children looked longingly at the couple that entered the orphanage, hoping to be chosen for adoption.

[He] belongs to an elite arm of the state police ... whose job it is to bail out those **hapless** adventurers who find more excitement than they reckoned on.[187]

For generations, Lassie has been America's family pet. Braving fierce currents, rescuing victims from burning buildings, befriending **hapless** animals and humans alike—the intelligent and gentle collie quickly became every man's best friend.[188]

write your own:

Hedonist

'hE-d&n-ist

(Noun) a pleasure seeking person
Keyword: He done it!

Fred is a **hedonist** who spray paints buildings for the fun of it. He doubles his pleasure by pointing to someone else and yelling, "**He done it!**"

Concerned only for herself and her own pleasures, Marilyn is considered a **hedonist**.

If eating, drinking and shopping your way through Taipei has made you feel like a hopeless **hedonist**, the new Museum of World Religions... offers a cool, calm space for introspection [examining one's thoughts].[185]

When [Noah Webster] penned the first American dictionary, in 1825, he defined happiness as "the agreeable sensations which spring from the enjoyment of good." That says it all. It has "agreeable sensations," the notion that happiness is a feeling. The **hedonists** would get off on that.[186]

write your own:

Heretic

'her-&-"tik

(Noun) a person who holds an opinion or belief that is against the principles of a particular religion

Keyword: hairy tick

He was considered a **heretic** because of his belief that no living creature should be killed, not even the **hairy tick** that suddenly appeared on his shoulder.

The **heretic** was removed from the ministry for his controversial doctrinal beliefs.

The drought was so dire by August that Aurora council members considered a near-**heretical** move—limiting water taps. That would mean limits on new housing and putting the brakes on the city's cherished growth.[187]

The Puritan authorities considered Quakers **heretics** and ordered them banished from Massachusetts.[188]

write your own:

Hone

'hOn

(Verb) to rub and sharpen/ to make something perfect or more suitable
Keyword: bone

The cavemen **honed** their skills by sharpening their **bones** into arrows.

In preparation for Thanksgiving dinner, dad **honed** the carving knife to a perfect point.

[He] went back to school in 1990 to **hone** his photography skills and, after amassing so many credits, decided to get a degree.[189]

Since the middle of the nineteen thirties, the city's best sleight-of-hand [a cleverly executed trick] men have been getting together every Saturday afternoon at one restaurant or another to talk shop and **hone** the niceties [precision] of their craft.[190]

write your own:

Impervious

im-'p&r-vE-&s or "im-'p&r-vE-&s
(Adjective) impossible to penetrate or affect
Keyword: emperor

The **emperor** was **impervious** to any bad news, showing no emotion.

The author was very proud of his first book and was **impervious** to any negative criticism.

Animals that scavenged for a living would also have enjoyed an advantage. Lizards were, and are, largely **impervious** to the bacteria in rotting carcasses.[197]

The most rigid structures, the most **impervious** to change, will collapse first.[198]

write your own:

Impetuous

im-'pech-w&s or im-'pe-ch-w&s

(Adjective) rash or impulsive
Keyword: a pet to us

The opossum became **a pet to us** after we made an **impetuous** decision at the last minute to rescue it from the local animal shelter.

He later regretted allowing the salesman to talk him into making an **impetuous** decision to buy a new car without selling his old one first.

[He was] described in court yesterday as "volatile and **impetuous**" and a "law unto herself...."[197]

Once awake, he made a number of snap judgments, some of them showing restraint and good sense, others demonstrating his sometimes **impetuous** nature.[198]

write your own:

http://SolidA.net ©Solid A, Inc. 137

Imprecation

"im-pri-'kA-sh&n

(Noun) a curse
Keyword: chimp vacation

The lab worker was angry and shouted all kinds of **imprecations** when he discovered that the lab had granted the monkeys a **chimp vacation**.

Because he chose to speak to his boss using **imprecations** when he was angry, he was suspended for one week without pay.

Outside court he enjoyed smoking cigars, quoting poetry, drinking claret ... in Pomeroy's Wine Bar and muttering **imprecations** against his domineering wife.[199]

Harrison won't help clean up [the] mess he allegedly helped create in Graham's room. Shouts, screams, **imprecations**. "You're an idiot!" "Shut up!" "I hate you!"[200]

write your own:

Impute

im-'pyüt

(Verb) to credit an action to a particular person or group
Keyword: chimp suit

The tailor was **imputed** in the **chimp suit** mix-up after the groom discovered that his tuxedo was mistakenly tailored for a chimp.

Environmentalists often **impute** global warming to corporations that are more interested in making money than taking care of their environment.

Readers often **impute** contrasting motives and conclusions to the same piece of journalism.[199]

At least it comes as no surprise to me; I prefer to **impute** as many everyday problems as possible to forces beyond my control....[200]

write your own:

i-'nAn

(Adjective) foolish or silly; lacking significance

Keyword: insane

The **inane** class clown was acting **insane** by standing on his head on the seat of his chair.

Bringing zoo animals to the birthday party was an **inane** idea as the animals ruined the expensive carpets and furniture.

That's just ridiculous. No reputable producer would ever do a show based on such an **inane** concept.[203]

Dreamcatcher is a moviegoer's nightmare. The story is incoherent [disorderly and confusing], **inane** and interminable [seemingly endless].[204]

write your own:

Incongruous

in-'kä[ng]-gr&-w&s

(Adjective) different from what generally happens/ inappropriate or out of place
Keyword: in Congress

The new representative looked very **incongruous** when he appeared **in Congress** without a shirt and with spiked hair.

Her unkempt room seemed **incongruous** in a house where everything was kept in perfect order.

Since a doctor who doesn't like sick people seems as **incongruous** as an investor who doesn't like risk, she began to question her chosen career.[201]

Most people have difficulty dealing with mixed messages of a verbal [spoken] nature. They are even more baffled by **incongruous** nonverbal ... messages.[202]

write your own: _____

Section 5 Crossword Puzzle

Across
1. having too much decoration; gaudy
3. talkative, usually about unimportant things
5. enjoying the company of others; outgoing
6. frantic; wildly excited; uncontrolled
8. to disregard or disobey intentionally
9. a curse
11. pleasure seeking
13. unlucky or unfortunate
14. to rub and sharpen/ to make something perfect or more suitable
16. rash or impulsive

Down
1. praise too positive to be considered sincere or genuine/ abundant
2. done secretly so as not to be noticed by others
4. to credit an action to a particular person or group
5. not required; uncalled for/ free or voluntary
6. to stir up or arouse
7. foolish or silly; lacking significance
10. impossible to penetrate or affect
12. different from what generally happens/ inappropriate or out of place
14. a person who holds an opinion or belief that is against a particular religion
15. trickery or deceit

Section 5 Multiple Choice Review

Select the word that best fits each sentence.

1. The travel agency created a slogan to attract _____: Take a vacation from your vacation and really have some fun.
   a. guile   b. heretics   c. hedonists   d. imprecations

2. The furniture maker was well known for the extra hours he spent adding _____ details to each piece of furniture.
   a. inane   b. imputed   c. florid   d. impetuous

3. Since losing much of his money at the casino and on the stock market, Bill has become a(n) _____, and somewhat solitary, man.
   a. garrulous   b. hapless   c. incongruous   d. gratuitous

4. I was worried when the grape juice spilled on the new table, but luckily, the tablecloth was _____ to liquid and nothing soaked through.
   a. hapless   b. impervious   c. incongruous   d. fulsome

5. After making her final decision she _____ bad taste to her friends who disagreed with her.
   a. fomented   b. imputed   c. flouted   d. honed

6. Martin Luther was once labeled a(n) _____, for his non-Catholic beliefs.
   a. hedonist   b. heretic   c. frenetic   d. flout

7. Even the reporters were unable to get a word in as the _____ speaker spoke rapidly without taking a breath.
   a. hapless   b. garrulous   c. gratuitous   d. hapless

8. Mark _____ his parents' rules by climbing out of his bedroom window to attend the party.
   a. flouted   b. imputed   c. honed   d. fomented

9. The televised surgery captured all of the _____ details, including close-ups of the incisions, blood and guts.
   a. hedonistic   b. impervious   c. gratuitous   d. furtive

10. The stirring picture was shown only for a minute on the news because it _____ such a strong emotion from the audience.
    a. fomented   b. honed   c. imputed   d. flouted

11. The Unabomber, who sent mail bombs protesting people using technology, was hard to catch as he led a _____ existence in a small cabin in Montana far away from anyone else.
    a. furtive   b. heretical   c. gregarious   d. fulsome

12. Although exhausting, the _____ week leading up to the wedding reception was well worth it; all the preparation definitely paid off.
    a. frenetic   b. fulsome   c. florid   d. hapless

13. After seeing the awful movie, I told myself I would never again believe any incredibly positive, _____ reviews from that movie critic again.
    a. impervious   b. fulsome   c. impetuous   d. gregarious

14. My cat is very _____ and doesn't like to be by himself.
    a. furtive   b. inane   c. gregarious   d. impetuous

15. Ruth Ann was considered to be trustworthy, lacking any _____.
    a. flout   b. foment   c. hone   d. guile

16. Frank enrolled in the advanced glass blowing course in order to _____ his glass blowing techniques.
    a. guile   b. foment   c. hone   d. impute

17. Many of Josh's friends fail to take him seriously due to his _____ sense of humor.
    a. hedonistic   b. florid   c. fulsome   d. inane

18. The new arts center looked strangely _____ in the impoverished section of town.
    a. inane   b. furtive   c. garrulous   d. incongruous

19. She had a very _____ personality when shopping and tended to make rash, and impulsive purchases.
    a. garrulous   b. florid   c. gratuitous   d. impetuous

20. Linda did not appreciate the _____ her teenage daughter used when she was with her friends.
    a. imprecations   b. guile   c. foment   d. flout

Section 5 Matching Review

Match the word on the left to the correct meaning on the right.

1. _____ Florid
2. _____ Flout
3. _____ Foment
4. _____ Frenetic
5. _____ Fulsome
6. _____ Furtive
7. _____ Garrulous
8. _____ Gratuitous
9. _____ Gregarious
10. _____ Guile
11. _____ Hapless
12. _____ Hedonist
13. _____ Heretic
14. _____ Hone
15. _____ Impervious
16. _____ Impetuous
17. _____ Imprecation
18. _____ Impute
19. _____ Inane
20. _____ Incongruous

A. not required; uncalled for/ free or voluntary
B. trickery or deceit
C. rash or impulsive
D. to credit an action to a particular person or group
E. a person who holds an opinion or belief that is against a particular religion
F. having too much decoration; gaudy
G. a curse
H. frantic; wildly excited; uncontrolled
I. done secretly so as not to be noticed by others
J. to disregard or disobey intentionally
K. praise too positive to be considered sincere or genuine/abundant
L. enjoying the company of others; outgoing
M. impossible to penetrate or affect
N. a pleasure seeking person
O. to stir up or arouse
P. to rub and sharpen/ to make something perfect or more suitable
Q. unlucky or unfortunate
R. easily deceived or tricked
S. talkative, usually about unimportant things
T. different from what generally happens/ inappropriate or out of place

Section Six

Incursion

in-'k&r-zh&n

(Noun) a sudden attack or entrance; a hostile invasion

Keyword: in cursive

The threat of the **incursion** was written **in cursive** handwriting. It said, "Surrender, or we will attack suddenly. Sincerely, the enemy."

Heidi's big brother made an **incursion** into the living room during the sleepover and scared the girls.

Crowded with comforting groups of pottery animals, enamel boxes and porcelain figurines, the room gave the impression of belonging to a woman trying to protect herself from the **incursions** of the outside world. —Princess Diana's room[203]

We are learning to regulate [govern] to allow for the freedoms the Internet was intended to provide us, while at the same time guard against undeserved **incursions** on our privacy, like the ones spammers make....[204]

write your own:

Indefatigable

"in-di-'fa-ti-g&-b&l

(Adjective) incapable of being tired
Keyword: in the fatigues

When he's **in the fatigues**, he is **indefatigable**--able to outlast all of the other soldiers during the drills.

Never giving up, he's been **indefatigable** in his quest to find a cure for cancer.

It soon became apparent that this schedule, even for the **indefatigable** Dr. Morton, was too demanding.[205]

The conquest of majestic Mount Everest caught the imagination of the world, bringing an unprecedented number of climbers each spring and fall. It also brought the Sherpas a generous and **indefatigable** benefactor [someone who does good to others] in the person of [Sir Edmund] Hillary.[206]

write your own:

Indolent

'in-d&-l&nt

(Adjective) habitually lazy or idle
Keyword: spindle bent

The **spindle bent** when the **indolent** movers dropped it down the stairs because they were too lazy to carry it.

Alex's **indolent** work habits led to very poor grades when he went to college.

Just as the **indolent** were not reprimanded [reproved or scolded], the best and the brightest—the teachers and principals who labored heroically against the odds—were neither rewarded nor commended [praised].[207]

The novelist ... reckons our obsession with sportswear is "an indication of the progressively more **indolent,** lazy, couch potato mentality of the great mass of people."[208]

write your own:

Indomitable

in-'dä-m&-t&-b&l

(Adjective) incapable of being conquered
Keyword: in dominoes

In dominoes he was the **indomitable** world champion—never losing a tournament.

The **indomitable** runner could not be kept from his workouts, not even if it was raining or snowing outside.

Seemingly **indomitable**, Microsoft boasts the best-selling suite, the best-selling Windows word processor, a highly competitive spreadsheet, and all the leverage of its operating system architecture and programming tools.[207]

The [Oakland] A's of 1999, you see, were much like this team—nearly **indomitable** at home, but profoundly iffy [unreliable] on the road.[208]

write your own:

Ingenuous

in-'jen-y&-w&s

(Adjective) displaying openness and simplicity often in a childlike manner; frank; naïve; trusting

Keyword: genuine

The jeweler spoke **ingenuously** about the **genuine** gems in the jewelry store, pointing out all the cracks and imperfections to his customers.

Margaret's friends had to watch out for her when they went places. She was so **ingenuous** they were afraid that someone would try to take advantage of her.

How unsuspecting, how **ingenuous** I've been. For weeks now I've been the dupe [fooled by] of a conspiracy.[209]

Human beings can build a magnificent reality in adulthood out of what was only an illusion in early childhood—their loving, joyous, trusting, **ingenuous**, unrealistic over idealization of their two parents.[210]

write your own:

Inimical

i-'ni-mi-k&l

(Adjective) hostile or unfriendly
Keyword: Indian nickel

The **inimical** coin collectors fought over the rare **Indian nickel**.

The landowners were **inimical** to anyone that tried to hunt on their land. They posted signs that read, "We shoot trespassers first and ask questions later."

The increased role of government has had many of the same adverse effects on higher education as on elementary and secondary education. It has fostered an atmosphere that both dedicated teachers and serious students often find **inimical** to learning.[209]

The mines were stable, not subject to cave-ins, and maintained a constant temperature and humidity that was not **inimical** to human comfort.[210]

write your own: _____

Innocuous

i-'nä-ky&-w&s

(Adjective) harmless; not dangerous or hostile
Keyword: inoculate

While the child was **inoculated** for Polio, the doctor explained how the shot was **innocuous** and would not really hurt him.

The **innocuous** looking miniature poodle was not as docile as it looked. It had been known to attack and bite unfamiliar people.

Although most heart murmurs are relatively **innocuous**, some have serious causes. If a murmur is detected, the doctor has to decide based on its nature if a further evaluation is warranted.[211]

Most of President Bush's overseas trips are carefully scripted and largely risk-free occasions, notable for smiling photo ops [opportunities] and **innocuous** official statements, not for difficult diplomacy.[212]

write your own:

Insolvent

in-'säl-v&nt or "in-'sol-v&nt

(Adjective) unable to pay debts; bankrupt
Keyword: solve

Unable to **solve** any mysteries the detective became **insolvent** and had to close his office.

The couple declared bankruptcy after finding out from their accountant they were **insolvent**.

Recently more than one hundred of America's wealthiest men and women who invested in the prestigious but now **insolvent** insurance company, Lloyd's of London, lost all their personal assets when their promissory notes to pay off Lloyd's debts were called in on a moment's notice.[213]

State legislators are expected to put the finishing touches today on a bill to provide an emergency $100-million state loan for the **insolvent** school district....[214]

write your own: _____

Intractable

in-'trak-t&-b&l or "in-'trak-t&-l

(Adjective) not easily managed or manipulated

Keyword: tractor

The **intractable tractor** refused to be operated by the farmer.

Romeo and Juliet could not solve the **intractable** problems between their families.

Find a cheap, renewable and clean form of energy ... [and many of the world's problems would] be solved. Yet [without] energy, many global problems remain **intractable**.[215]

It would be easy to conclude that cement is a rotten business and accept high costs, slow growth, and customer dissatisfaction ... But starting in the early 1990s, new leadership realized that solving these seemingly **intractable** problems would give [them] a unique position in the industry.[216]

write your own:

Intransigence (also intransigeance)
in-'tran-s&-j&ns or in-'trant-s&-j&nts

(Noun) refusal to come to an agreement or compromise
Keyword: in a trance again

The hypnotist avoided any **intransigence** with his customers. If they would not agree to pay, he put them **in a trance again**.

Due to the angry workers' **intransigence**, their union refused to agree on a settlement.

Toan denied that he was financing the Jesuits' covert [secret] operation in Japan, but steadfastly refused to abjure [give up] his faith. Such **intransigence** infuriated the authorities....[215]

Their continued **intransigence** has done their members a serious disservice, and surely leaves the government with no choice but to impose a settlement....[216]

write your own:

Intrepid

in-'tre-p&d

(Adjective) fearless or adventurous
Keyword: in trap

The **intrepid** explorer caught a fierce polar bear **in a trap**.

The **intrepid** rock climber constantly searched for more challenging places to climb.

So when it was put to him that there might be scientific and political value in sending a party to explore the interior of America beyond the Mississippi he leapt at the idea, hoping the **intrepid** adventurers would find herds of healthy mastodons ... grazing on the bounteous plains. [regarding Lewis and Clark's famous expedition][217]

On May 29, 1953, at 11: 30 on a blustery morning, the two **intrepid** souls [Sir Edmund Hillary and Tenzing Norgay] stood side by side, about 29,000 feet above sea level [on Mt. Everest].[218]

write your own:

Inure

i-'nur or i-'nyur

(Verb) to become used to something unpleasant; to harden
Keyword: a lure

The lousy fisherman got **a lure** caught in his back so many times he became **inured** to the painful process of having it removed.

After serving years in the prison cell, the prisoner became **inured** to hardships.

War Admiral [a racing horse] was a raging lion behind the gate, and Smith was concerned that Seabiscuit would take one look at his opponent's tantrum and throw one of his own. He needed to expose Seabiscuit to a similarly unruly gate horse and **inure** him to the sight of it.[219]

Its purpose, much like the physical beatings, is to **inure** the senses to insult [hardship], to harden the will against responding with rage and fear....[220]

write your own:

Irascible

i-'ra-s&-b&l

(Adjective) easily provoked or angered
Keyword: harass

Due to Jane's quick temper and **irascible** nature, students thought it was funny to **harass** her.

As Cindy's daughter grew into a teenager, she became more volatile and **irascible** than ever.

He rarely gives interviews, but when he does, he's about the bluntest, most **irascible**, most straight-talkin' guy out there.[221]

Unusually clever for a white dragon, [he] has a personality like an icy, rusted blade. He is **irascible**, unpleasant, and thoroughly evil. [222]

write your own:

Lachrymose
'la-kr&-"mOs

(Adjective) sad; given easily to tears
Keyword: lack the most

The child that **lacked the most** toys was **lachrymose** and began to cry.

The **lachrymose** puppy whined and cried every time its owners left it alone.

Referring to his involuntary retirement in 1964, he claimed the manner of his going as a proud achievement. He was not referring to his **lachrymose** farewell speech at the party... that gave him his marching orders [orders to leave or move on].[225]

Canadian Counter-tenor Matthew White "reclaims" the work here to open his excellent recital of elegiac [sorrowful], **lachrymose** music from the 17th and 18th Centuries.[226]

write your own:

Laconic

l&-'kä-nik

(Adjective) using few words; concise
Keyword: lack of

Because the driver was **laconic**, the passenger complained about the **lack of** communication during the long trip.

He opened his mouth just enough to let out a few **laconic** remarks.

He has never joined any group, party, or discussion in any way other than silently. Stealth is in his nature. He is **laconic** and cautious and light on his feet.[225]

Volz is a curious combination of reticence [keeping to one's self] and daring, unafraid to leap brashly [boldly or audaciously] off catwalks [platforms] 55 feet high in Indiana's field house but **laconic** even with his good friends.[226]

write your own:

Lassitude

'la-s&-"tüd or 'la-s&-"tyüd

(Noun) physical or mental weariness; sluggishness
Keyword: lasso dude

While performing in the rodeo, **Lasso Dude** was overcome by a feeling of **lassitude** and was unable to finish his performance.

After completing the marathon, a feeling of **lassitude** overcame the runners.

If one word sums up a constellation of reactions in a myriad of towns, villages and cities at the end of the war, it is **lassitude**. Exhaustion was the prevailing feeling after four-and-a-half years of carnage [destruction].[227]

The first Matrix [a movie] succeeded in making alienation captivating: It proposed that the everyday world of the late 20th century was the creation of conquering machines that numbed humans into **lassitude**, then fed off their bioelectrical force.[228]

write your own:

Lionize

'lI-&-"nIz

(Verb) to treat as a celebrity
Keyword: lion

The **lion** was **lionized** after playing the lead role in the most popular movie in the jungle and was treated like a celebrity.

At the piano recital, the young girl was **lionized** for her exceptional performance. One small child even asked for her autograph.

Canadian photographers lined up to **lionize** Yousuf Karsh last night as the eminent [famous] Canadian portrait shooter [photographer].[229]

While journalists **lionize** the goal scorer ... "coaches must find ways to break down this traditional and simple analysis"—often by highlighting the less eye-catching lead-up work of teammates.[230]

write your own:

Loquacious

lO-'kwA-sh&s

(Adjective) talking excessively
Keyword: locust

The **loquacious locust** talked so much that the other bugs stopped listening.

The **loquacious** professor rarely allowed his students to ask a question, let alone get a word in edgewise.

The **loquacious** private shareholder known for taking the microphone at annual meetings with a string of questions ranging from the political to the pedantic [academic], is moving into top gear.[231]

Still, the many clips transport us to the time when Paar personified must-see TV on NBC, with his rambling, personal monologues [a one-person show] as well as free-flowing conversation that proved the **loquacious** host was also a superior listener.[232]

write your own: _____

http://SolidA.net ©Solid A, Inc. 165

Lugubrious

lu-'gü-brE-&s or lu-'gyü-brE-&s

(Adjective) mournful or very sad/ dismal
Keyword: love glue

Cherie felt **lugubrious** when all of her friends received a dose of **love glue** from cupid, and she was somehow overlooked.

The child was **lugubrious** after her puppy ran away from home and nothing could console her.

I saw tears on the faces of many former Rebels. Even Mrs. Shau looked **lugubrious**. They had a mask for every occasion.[233]

There they stood as the [hockey] game ended, with Tikkanen wearing his trademark manic grin, Gretzky the **lugubrious** look of an unwilling dance partner.[234]

write your own:

Maladroit

"ma-l&-'droit

(Adjective) clumsy or bumbling; awkward
Keyword: mail android (as in a robot that delivers mail)

The **maladroit mail android** was so clumsy he was unable to get the mail into the mailboxes.

The **maladroit** cowboy made a hilarious rodeo clown where his clumsy and awkward nature was a natural fit for the job.

My sister asked me to review a video game for her 8-year-old son, something she can't do herself, because she's technologically **maladroit**....[235]

[He] can give a dynamite presentation to a big audience, but seems awkward in groups and **maladroit** at small talk.[236]

write your own:

Section 6 Crossword Puzzle

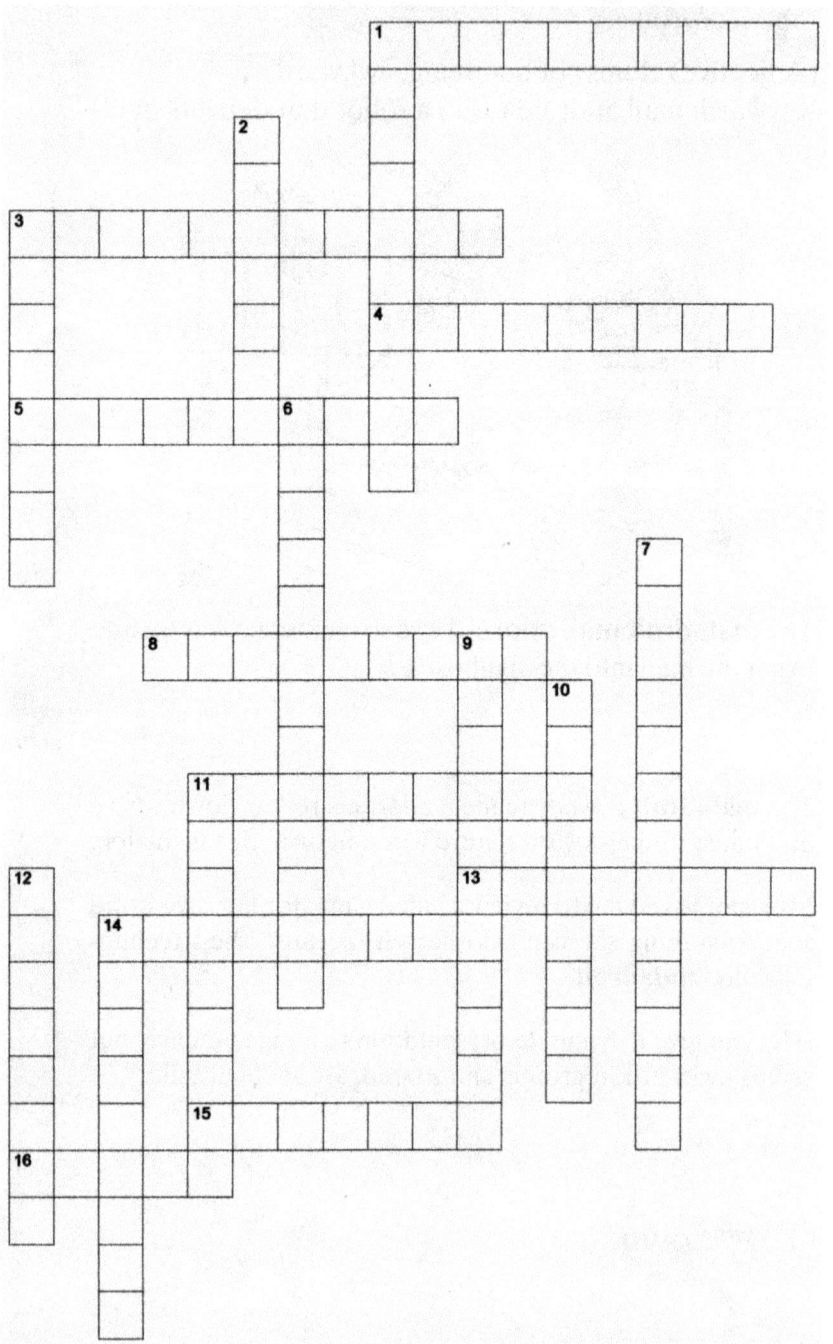

Across

1. sad; given easily to tears
3. not easily managed or manipulated
4. a sudden attack or entrance; a hostile invasion
5. talking excessively
8. clumsy or bumbling; awkward
11. displaying openness and simplicity often in a childlike manner; frank; naïve; trusting
13. hostile or unfriendly
14. unable to pay debts; bankrupt
15. to treat as a celebrity
16. to become used to something unpleasant; to harden

Down

1. mournful or very sad/ dismal
2. using few words; concise
3. habitually lazy or idle
6. incapable of being tired
7. refusal to come to an agreement or compromise
9. incapable of being conquered
10. physical or mental weariness; sluggishness
11. easily provoked or angered
12. fearless or adventurous
14. harmless; not dangerous or hostile

Section 6 Multiple Choice Review

Select the word that best fits each sentence.

1. Part of the downfall of the economy is due to people losing their jobs, making them _____ as consumers.
   a. insolvent   b. intrepid   c. indefatigable   d. intractable

2. Ken was a(n) _____ tennis player. Not only was he clumsy, he also hit most of the tennis balls over the fence.
   a. maladroit   b. indomitable   c. lachrymose   d. ingenuous

3. Roger's boss fired him for his _____ attitude toward work when he caught Roger sitting down on the job again.
   a. intrepid   b. innocuous   c. ingenuous   d. indolent

4. The student's oral report seemed rather _____, and fell far short of the required time.
   a. loquacious   b. maladroit   c. laconic   d. lugubrious

5. The movie was so sad that the audience left the theater feeling _____.
   a. laconic   b. irascible   c. indefatigable   d. lugubrious

6. The telemarketer was _____ to constant rejection and was able to ignore rude people.
   a. inimical   b. inured   c. lionized   d. indolent

7. The kids look up to their dad as a(n) _____ fire fighter who is the strongest, bravest man in the world.
   a. indomitable   b. indolent   c. insolvent   d. inimical

8. The new renters were _____ and prone to fighting other people in their apartment complex.
   a. indomitable   b. inimical   c. innocuous   d. indolent

9. _____ conflicts, like the feud between the Hatfields and McCoys, often take generations to solve.
   a. lugubrious   b. insolvent   c. innocuous   d. intractable

10. The Venus flytrap seems completely _____ to unsuspecting flies, until they get too close.
    a. intractable   b. inimical   c. innocuous   d. inure

11. The prisoner was so moody and _____ that the guards were afraid to speak to him.
    a. irascible   b. laconic   c. maladroit   d. intractable

12. Susan is so _____ that nearly anything will set her off crying.
    a. loquacious   b. irascible   c. lachrymose   d. intrepid

13. The car salesman tried very hard to reverse the couple's decision about which car they were going to buy, but their _____ was immovable.
    a. intransigence   b. lassitude   c. incursion   d. indolence

14. After studying for the test for many hours, Paul felt a great sense of _____ and wanted to get some rest.
    a. lionization   b. lassitude   c. intransigence   d. lugubriousness

15. Cameron was _____ as the local hero after rescuing a child from a burning building.
    a. inured   b. indomitable   c. innocuous   d. lionized

16. The hairdresser is very _____; she talks non-stop to her customers for hours.
    a. lugubrious   b. ingenuous   c. lachrymose   d. loquacious

17. Seven years after leaving the orphanage, the _____ search for her twin sister paid off.
    a. indolent   b. indomitable   c. indefatigable   d. insolvent

18. A moat was built around the castle to help ward off any further enemy _____.
    a. intransigence   b. maladroits   c. incursions   d. insolvents

19. Because he appeared too naïve and trusting, the _____ young man was mugged in the subway.
    a. loquacious   b. indefatigable   c. ingenuous   d. lassitude

20. The _____ firefighters remained calm as the fire unexpectedly flared up and changed direction.
    a. intrepid   b. lionized   c. laconic   d. irascible

Section 6 Matching Review

Match the word on the left to the correct meaning on the right.

1. _____ Incursion
2. _____ Indefatigable
3. _____ Indolent
4. _____ Indomitable
5. _____ Ingenuous
6. _____ Inimical
7. _____ Innocuous
8. _____ Insolvent
9. _____ Intractable
10. _____ Intransigence
11. _____ Intrepid
12. _____ Inure
13. _____ Irascible
14. _____ Lachrymose
15. _____ Laconic
16. _____ Lassitude
17. _____ Lionize
18. _____ Loquacious
19. _____ Lugubrious
20. _____ Maladroit

A. easily provoked or angered
B. fearless or adventurous
C. unable to pay debts; bankrupt
D. incapable of being tired
E. talking excessively
F. harmless; not dangerous or hostile
G. refusal to come to an agreement or compromise
H. clumsy or bumbling; awkward
I. a sudden attack or entrance; a hostile invasion
J. sad; given easily to tears
K. using few words; concise
L. physical or mental weariness; sluggishness
M. incapable of being conquered
N. displaying openness and simplicity often in a childlike manner; frank; naïve; trusting
O. to treat as a celebrity
P. not easily managed or manipulated
Q. mournful or very sad/ dismal
R. hostile or unfriendly
S. to become used to something unpleasant; to harden
T. habitually lazy or idle

Section Seven

Malevolent

m&-'le-v&-l&nt

(Adjective) ill-willed/ causing evil or harm to others
Keyword: [shopping] mall devil

The **malevolent** "**Mall Devil**" caused bad things to happen to the shoppers.

His reputation as a **malevolent** person made me leery of being his friend.

Plunging through 2 feet of water to her office stairs, she saw all around her evidence of nature's **malevolent** power.[237]

The pit's **malevolent** red eye—obscured [hidden] by gases and a balcony ledge of new volcanic rock—sits just a few hundred feet below.[238]

write your own:

Melancholy

'me-l&n-"kä-lE

(Noun) sadness or depression
(Adjective) sad or gloomy
Keyword: melon collie

Because our dog devoured all of the melons in the garden when he felt sad and **melancholy**, we nicknamed him **"Melon Collie."**

After a few months, his **melancholy** demeanor was beginning to affect the attitudes of his close friends, making them feel blue.

A queenless colony [of bees] is a pitiful and **melancholy** community; there may be a mournful wail or lament from within... Without intervention, the colony will die. [239]

He had no energy, and the bigger he got, the less he played. Sluggishness eventually weighted him to the lawn chair and tending the grill, where he cooked burgers and ribs, and drank longneck beers with a twist of **melancholy**. [240]

write your own: _____

http://SolidA.net   ©Solid A, Inc.

Mendicant

'men-di-k&nt

(Noun) a beggar
Keyword: mending can

She gave out **mending cans** to all the **mendicants** on the street, hoping they would sew the holes in their clothes.

The volunteers worked like **mendicants**, begging strangers for donations for the new church.

While there are no laws against begging in Jerusalem, the police and the municipality continue to be at loggerheads [quarrelsome disagreement] over which of their departments is responsible for regulating the **mendicants'** activities.[241]

For [former United Kingdom Prime Minister] Churchill's part there was the detestation [extreme dislike] that is often felt by the **mendicant**; he hated having to be polite to the man he was asking for a loan.[242]

write your own:

Mnemonic

ni-'mä-nik

(Adjective) assisting the memory
Keyword: new mom

The **new mom** used **mnemonic** devices to remember the names of her newborn octuplets.

Chad discovered that using **mnemonic** devices to study for the test was the best way to remember the material.

Another enduring **mnemonic** is how to tell the difference between stalactites and stalagmites [rock formations in caves]: stalactites hang on tight to make sure they don't fall off; stalagmites try with all their might to grow upwards.[241]

To ignite your memory power, try the following **mnemonic** techniques. Trigger words. Instead of trying to remember an entire story or speech word-for-word, use a few word cues.[242]

write your own:

Multifarious

"m&l-t&-'far-E-&s

(Adjective) characterized by great variety or diversity
Keyword: multiple Ferris Wheels

Multiple Ferris Wheels of all shapes and sizes became a **multifarious** attraction at the fair.

The convention drew a **multifarious** crowd with diverse occupations and backgrounds.

The world's top club competition, the Club Cup brings together the best teams from the **multifarious** leagues in Europe....[245]

In his famous essay ... the poet suggests that the "monotony of the Dutch landscape gave rise to dreams of **multifarious**, colorful, and unusual flora [vegetation]."[246]

write your own:

Munificence

myu-'ni-f&-s&nts or myu-'ni-f&-s&ns

(Noun) the quality of being extremely generous
Keyword: new fifty cents

When the **new fifty cent** pieces were first introduced, the **munificent** coin collector gave away thousands out of generosity.

The town rapturously thanked Paul Newman for his **munificence**. Due to his generous donations, the town was able to rebuild after being destroyed by a tornado.

[I will] appease him with all **munificence**. Here before everyone I may enumerate the gifts I'll give. Seven new tripods and ten bars of gold, then twenty shining caldrons, and twelve horses....[243]

Do we want to contemplate his **munificence**? We see it in the abundance with which he fills the earth.[244]

write your own:

Nadir

'nA-d&r or 'nA-"dir

(Noun) worst moment; the lowest point

Keyword: gator

The **gator** reached his **nadir** when he was caught and transported to the zoo.

The **nadir** of my life was the day my car was wrecked, my girlfriend broke up with me, and I tripped and broke my leg.

The 2002 election marked the modern **nadir** of the Democratic Party in Colorado. Republicans wrestled the state Senate from the Democrats, retained control of the House and re-elected Bill Owens governor.[247]

The glory was a long time coming for the Dayton Flyers, a proud basketball program that had gone 17-67 in a three-season **nadir** from 1992 to 1995.[248]

write your own:

Nascent

'na-s&nt or 'nA-s&nt

(Adjective) starting to develop, recently started, or brand new
Keyword: NASA sent

NASA sent a **nascent** research module with the latest technological innovations to the international space station.

The **nascent** tree was well known for how much fruit it produced just months after being planted.

He shifted the attaché case to his left hand and was aware of the book, like a tumor, he thought, **nascent** at the moment, newly discovered, awaiting diagnosis.[245]

There is a **nascent** effort to translate emotional skills into software that will "humanize" computers.[246]

write your own: _____

http://SolidA.net ©Solid A, Inc.

Nefarious

ni-'far-E-&s or ni-'fer-E-&s

(Adjective) evil or wicked
Keyword: not far

When the **nefarious** queen, scheming to kill Snow White, asked the enchanted mirror where she was, the mirror replied, "**Not far**."

It was recently uncovered that the company had been participating in **nefarious** activities and that the owner was the head of the mafia.

These lawmakers fear information readily available in government records can be used for **nefarious** reasons, including terrorist attacks, identity theft, fraud, and invasion of privacy.[247]

Tropico 2 lets you don [put on] an eye patch and wooden leg to control a Caribbean island full of **nefarious** buccaneers [pirates].[248]

write your own:

Obfuscate

'äb-f&-"skAt or äb-'f&s-"kAt

(Verb) to make something more difficult to understand; to obscure
Keyword: office skate

The introduction of "**office skates**" into the work area resulted in a terrific mess that mixed up and **obfuscated** the reports and files.

The technical vocabulary in the manual **obfuscated** the instructions, resulting in an extra hour of assembly.

The book's main weakness is that the arguments are not always cogently [convincingly] expressed and sometimes **obfuscate** rather than clarify the issues—a common weakness of works written by academics for academics.[253]

The highest profile male in the women's game, didn't flinch, dodge or **obfuscate** when the question was put to him recently: "Are male coaches in women's basketball in danger of going the way of the dinosaur?"[254]

write your own: _____

Obsequious

&b-'sE-kwE-&s or äb -'sE-kwE-&s

(Adjective) too willing to serve or obey; servile; overly submissive

Keyword: sequins

The mean step-mother dressed in **sequins**, wished her step-daughter was more **obsequious**. She should not only want to do all the servile work in the house, but she should be happy doing it.

A marriage counselor recommended that if Robert wanted to save his marriage, he should cultivate a more **obsequious** attitude toward his wife and let her take charge sometimes.

"That book doesn't have fifty words in it that were changed by the editor!" exclaimed one author. "They were so respectful of my judgment, they were **obsequious**," said another.[255]

He began by writing an **obsequious** letter to Hitler, hailing him as "the great designer of German existence."[256]

write your own:

Obstreperous

&b-'stre-p&-r&s or äb-'stre-pr&s

(Adjective) noisy and difficult to deal with; defiant
Keyword: step on us

Their last words were, "Don't **step on us**," but the **obstreperous** monster was defiant and refused to obey.

The waitress decided to give the incoming party a table in the back of the restaurant because she knew they had a tendency to be noisy and **obstreperous**.

In the midst of the week-long debate, Lawrence, who had been on his best behavior, began to revert to his old ways. When, becoming **obstreperous**, he made an impudent [sassy] remark, no one knew what to say.[253]

Now suppose there are parents who are **obstreperous**, cranky, and argumentative, who insist on running the household and refuse to hand over anything....[254]

write your own: _____

Officious

&-'fi-sh&s

(Adjective) eager to give advice or services when they are not wanted; meddlesome
Keyword: official

The **officious official** kept interfering in the basketball game to give the players advice.

The teenage girl felt that her parents were rather **officious** when they read her diary and listened to her phone conversations.

They defied the **officious** ushers who tried to keep them in their cushioned seats, erupting at the slightest shout or hip twitch from the minister of the New Super Heavy Funk.[255]

A veritable [authentic] army of auctioneers from the National Auction Group of Gadsden, Alabama, all wearing matching American-flag ties, were doing their **officious** best to prod, prod, prod.[256]

write your own:

Opulent

'ä-py&-l&nt

(Adjective) rich or wealthy
Keyword: opal

The **opulent** movie star showed off her wealth by wearing lots of **opal** jewels.

The **opulent** hotel was decorated with lots of fresh flowers, luxurious fabrics, and dark, rich paint to create a grand feeling for the customers.

Air Force families had fond memories of a charming country peopled by strange yet amiable [friendly] folk, affording an **opulent** lifestyle replete with luxurious homes, servants, and nannies....[257]

Neither side is immoral, unless their values get pushed to an excess of **opulent** indulgence on one hand or miserly bargain-driving on the other.[258]

write your own:

Ossify

'ä-s&-"fI

(Verb) to become rigid or fixed in place; to become bone; to become set in one's ways

Keyword: office fly

After months of being stuck on the glue strip, the **office fly ossified** and became rock hard.

The professor's teaching methods had become so outdated and **ossified** that he was no longer able to relate to his students.

They blame local authority employers for allowing terms and conditions to **ossify** over 25 years, during which the Fire Brigades Union refused to discuss changes to outdated working practices.[259]

The dried-up creek bed didn't just have one color, it had dozens, all combinations of the basic four colors—dark red hematite, lemon yellow, white pipeclay and black manganese that looked like chewing gum spat out by dinosaurs and left to **ossify**. The colored stones and pebbles were strewn in every direction.[260]

write your own:

Palliate

'pa-lE-"At

(Verb) to make something appear less serious than it is relieve without curing
Keyword: pal ate

Our **pal ate** a gallon of ice cream to **palliate** the pain he felt after being turned down for a date.

Attempting to **palliate** her boy's fears after he fell down, the mother covered up the scrape on his leg so he couldn't see the blood.

They are too embarrassed to confess their sins [openly], lest their confessors should think less of them, so they **palliate** them and make them appear less evil, and thus it is to excuse themselves rather than to accuse themselves that they go to confession.[263]

Attired in an old army coat worn in the Mexican War and a broken-visored V.M.I. cadet Captain Jackson constantly sucked lemons to **palliate** his dyspepsia [indigestion] and refused to season his food with pepper because (he said) it made his left leg ache.[264]

write your own:

Panegyric

"pa-n&-'jir-ik or "pa-n&-'jI-rik

(Noun) a formal, elaborate speech of praise

Keyword: pen of lyrics

The **pen of lyrics** sings **panegyric** praises and affirmations to increase your self-esteem.

The **panegyric** in the paper praised the new editor for his accomplishments and qualifications.

The Secret History—so named by Chinese archivists [keepers of historical documents—seems to be more than a **panegyric** written to enhance [Genghis Khan's] reputation.[265]

There was no sarcasm intended, it being part of a longer **panegyric**.[266]

write your own:

Paradigm

'par-&-"dIm or 'par-&-"dim

(Noun) a model or an example/a way of thinking
Keyword: pair of dimes

The introduction of the **pair of dimes** to the natives began a new **paradigm** for their trading.

Copernicus developed a new astronomical **paradigm** describing how the earth and other planets move around the sun.

Technologists, like scientists, tend to hold on to their theories until incontrovertible [not able to refute] evidence, usually in the form of failures, convinces them to accept new **paradigms**.[261]

Zizek does clever things with the paradoxes [contradictions] inherent in this situation, but in the end he is reduced to arguing that people don't need another **paradigm**; they just need to act, to break out of the box of received ideas, and meaning will take care of itself.[262]

write your own: _____

Pariah

p&-'rI-&

(Noun) an outcast
Keyword: parade

The **pariah** was **paraded** through the streets on his way to jail.

When the spy was discovered selling secrets, he became a **pariah** in the eyes of his country.

The boys there have ostracized [excluded] him for his vanity and self-absorption, and he is a **pariah**.[263]

He won his seat in 1992 by unseating a well-liked incumbent [an official who holds an office] who was the GOP [Grand Old Party - Republicans] caucus' only woman, and the following year became a **pariah** after breaking with every Republican colleague by voting against a spending plan that raised taxes.[264]

write your own:

Parsimony

'pär-s&-"mO-nE

(Noun) being stingy or excessively careful with one's money
Keyword: purse of money

The children accused the mother of **parsimony**: she had a **purse of money** but refused to buy them any toys.

For reasons of **parsimony**, Mary decided to buy an older model car that was more affordable.

A major stumbling block has been money. Donor fatigue and **parsimony** have led to major shortfalls in funds for control programs.[267]

Instead of practical wisdom, such as "A penny saved is a penny earned," we are given **parsimonious** exhortations [advice] to transform dryer lint into Halloween costumes.[268]

write your own: _____

Section 7 Crossword Puzzle

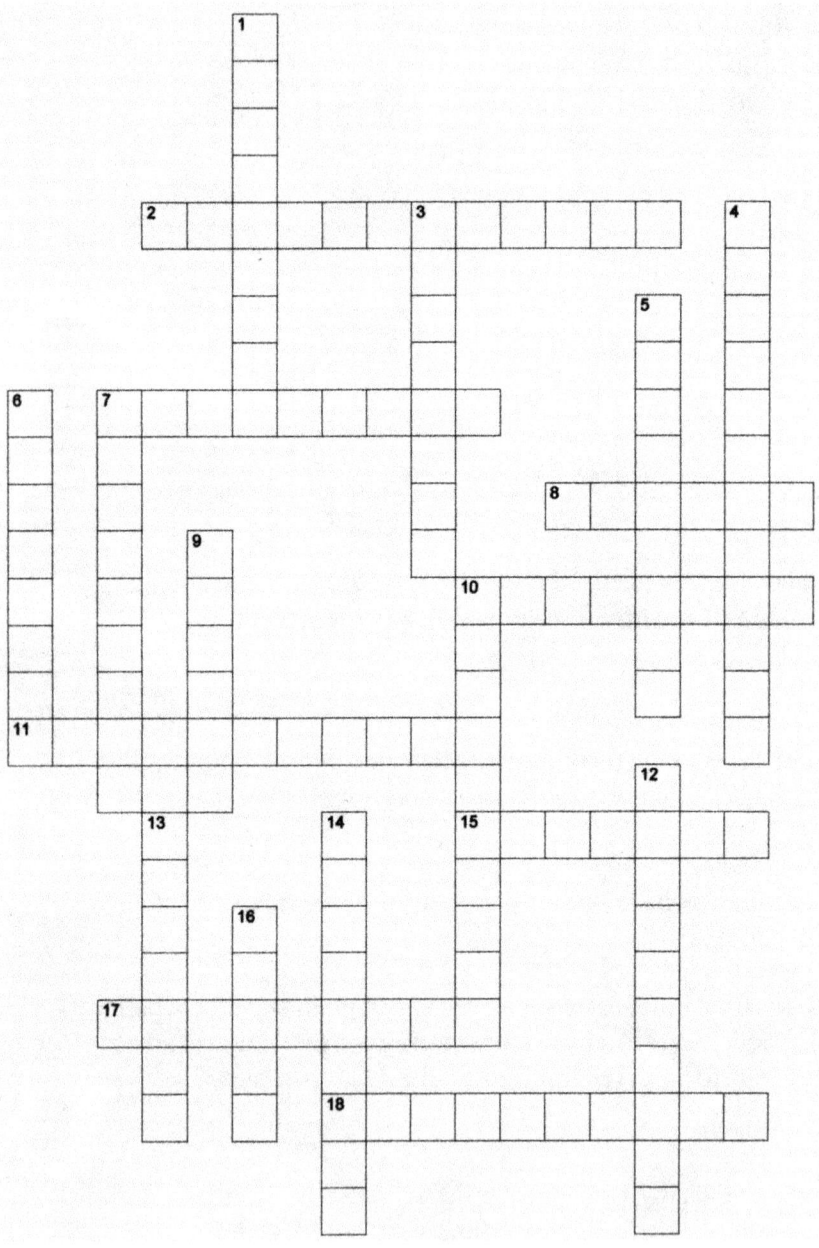

Across

2. noisy and difficult to deal with; defiant
7. a formal, elaborate speech of praise
8. an outcast
10. assisting the memory
11. the quality of being extremely generous
15. rich or wealthy
17. a beggar
18. too willing to serve or obey; servile; overly submissive

Down

1. to make something more difficult to understand; to obscure
3. to make something appear less serious than it is/ relieve without curing
4. characterized by great variety or diversity
5. evil or wicked
6. a model or an example/ a way of thinking
7. being stingy or excessively careful with one's money
9. to become rigid or fixed in place/ to become bone
10. ill-willed/ causing evil or harm to others
12. sadness or depression/ sad or gloomy
13. starting to develop, recently started, or brand new
14. eager to give advice or services when they are not wanted; meddlesome
16. worst moment; the lowest point

Section 7 Multiple Choice Review

Select the word that best fits each sentence.

1. Because of his _____ reputation in the community, no one was surprised when he was arrested for the local homicide.
   a. mnemonic   b. parsimonious   c. obsequious   d. nefarious

2. The infomercial bragged about the _____ product not yet available at stores.
   a. obsequious   b. opulent   c. nascent   d. officious

3. The music of The Rolling Stones appeals to a(n) _____ audience of all ages and races.
   a. nascent   b. nefarious   c. multifarious   d. obstreperous

4. Being defeated in the talent contest was the _____ of Chris's musical career.
   a. paradigm   b. pariah   c. nadir   d. nascent

5. The other kids made John a(n) _____, refusing to play with him because he smelled bad.
   a. mendicant   b. paradigm   c. pariah   d. panegyric

6. The student's _____ and argumentative nature made him a perfect candidate for the debate team.
   a. opulent   b. obstreperous   c. melancholy   d. multifarious

7. The book was criticized for _____ the issue it was advertised to clarify.
   a. palliating   b. obfuscating   c. ossifying   d. nadir

8. The family's _____ lifestyle was partially intended to make their neighbors jealous.
   a. officious   b. opulent   c. malevolent   d. multifarious

9. Because she was so eager to help out, her _____ work ethic helped her earn a promotion at her job much faster than most of her co-workers.
   a. malevolent   b. nascent   c. obsequious   d. obstreperous

10. After losing their parents, the poor children had no option but to beg for food like _____ .
    a. pariahs   b. mendicants   c. paradigms   d. nadirs

11. In the engineering class, students were encouraged to think beyond the old _____ to develop a new mechanism that runs on an alternative energy source.
    a. pariahs   b. munificence   c. nadirs   d. paradigms

12. After the cast was placed on his leg, the bone took several months to _____ .
    a. ossify   b. obfuscate   c. parsimony   d. palliate

13. Maria's doctor prescribed aspirin to _____ the pain in her foot.
    a. ossify   b. nadir   c. palliate   d. obfuscate

14. The best man's _____ at the wedding reception was sentimental and told of some of his favorite times with the groom.
    a. munificence   b. pariah   c. parsimony   d. panegyric

15. For reasons of _____, the college students chose not to turn on their air conditioners on hot days, using fans instead.
    a. parsimony   b. munificence   c. opulence   d. malevolence

16. The _____ police man asked the speeding driver all types of prodding questions into his personal life before giving him a ticket.
    a. multifarious   b. officious   c. obsequious   d. mendicant

17. Although she had no _____ intentions, she caused a great deal of harm by having the local animal shelter shut down.
    a. malevolent   b. mnemonic   c. multifarious   d. melancholy

18. In order for her students to learn the fifty states more quickly, the teacher developed _____ sayings for them to rehearse.
    a. mnemonic   b. malevolent   c. panegyric   d. nefarious

19. Her _____ behavior after giving birth was diagnosed as postpartum depression.
    a. officious   b. melancholy   c. malevolent   d. nefarious

20. A grand banquet was given to thank the donors for their _____ .
    a. paradigms   b. munificence   c. panegyrics   d. parsimony

Section 7 Matching Review

Match the word on the left to the correct meaning on the right.

1. ____ Malevolent
2. ____ Melancholy
3. ____ Mendicant
4. ____ Mnemonic
5. ____ Multifarious
6. ____ Munificence
7. ____ Nadir
8. ____ Nascent
9. ____ Nefarious
10. ____ Obfuscate
11. ____ Obsequious
12. ____ Obstreperous
13. ____ Officious
14. ____ Opulent
15. ____ Ossify
16. ____ Palliate
17. ____ Panegyric
18. ____ Paradigm
19. ____ Pariah
20. ____ Parsimony

A. ill-willed/ causing evil or harm to others
B. the quality of being extremely generous
C. too willing to serve or obey; servile; overly submissive
D. an outcast
E. rich or wealthy
F. being stingy or excessively careful with one's money
G. assisting the memory
H. noisy and difficult to deal with; defiant
I. a formal, elaborate speech of praise
J. characterized by great variety or diversity
K. to make something more difficult to understand; to obscure
L. starting to develop, recently started, or brand new
M. a model or an example/ a way of thinking
N. sadness or depression/ sad or gloomy
O. eager to give advice or services when they are not wanted; meddlesome
P. to make something appear less serious than it is/ relieve without curing
Q. to become rigid or fixed in place/ to become bone
R. evil or wicked
S. a beggar
T. worst moment; the lowest point

Section Eight

Paucity

'po-s&-tE

(Noun) scarcity or lack of number
Keyword: paw city (as in the paw of an animal)

In **Paw City** there is a **paucity** of people, but many animals.

Cowboys had to dance by themselves because of the **paucity** of women in the old west.

The most alarming aspect of New York's plan is that the Rangers have been left with a **paucity** of quality players between the ages of 24 and 29—the young veterans who form the core of many NHL teams on the rise.[269]

Many possible causes of the second Comet crash were put forward, but no conclusion could be reached with the **paucity** of evidence available.[270]

write your own:

Pellucid

p&-'lü-s&d

(Adjective) transparent; clear
Keyword: polluted

Over time the transparent water in the **pellucid** lake became **polluted** and murky.

After the window was cleaned, it was once again **pellucid** and helped to brighten the room.

The desert storm is over and through the pure sweet **pellucid** air the cliff swallows and the nighthawks plunge and swerve, making cries of hunger and warning....[267]

Downstream, [they] found themselves in a midday rise, trout leaving the stream bed—every spot and speckle visible in the **pellucid** water and bright sunlight—to intercept mayflies hatching out on the surface.[268]

write your own:

Peregrinate

'per-&-gr&-"nAt

(Verb) to wander or travel from place to place
Keyword: pair of grenades

Stuck with a **pair of grenades**, the soldier **peregrinated** for miles, searching for a safe spot to detonate them.

The group **peregrinated** several kilometers down the main street to display their signs and demonstrate their dedication to the cause.

I asked if she didn't think it insufferable that a 10-year-old should be pressed to provide official documentation to travel from one city to another. She looked at me sharply: "Doesn't your son have a passport?"
[She replied] "To **peregrinate** within our native homeland?"[271]

Join the thousands of music lovers from all over the world who **peregrinate** to the Delta Blues Museum, located in an 1812 train depot at the edge of town.[272]

write your own:

Perfidious

p&r-'fi-dE-&s or "p&r-'fi-dE-&s

(Adjective) treacherous; not trustworthy
Keyword: hideous

The **perfidious** villain had a **hideous** face that could not be trusted.

The zoo caretakers had to be careful, especially when feeding the tigers. They were considered **perfidious** and extremely dangerous when hungry.

According to his ex-wife … 50 years after their marriage, he was rude and **perfidious**.[269]

When our nation is at war with any other, we detest them under the character of cruel, **perfidious**, unjust and violent: But always esteem ourselves and allies equitable, moderate, and merciful.[270]

write your own: _____

_____

Perfunctory

p&r-'f&[ng]k-t&-rE

(Adjective) performed without care or interest/ done automatically
Keyword: purr factory

Adding the purr to the toy kittens at the **purr factory** was a **perfunctory** job that the workers could do with their eyes closed.

She read the book in such a **perfunctory** manner that the book club members thought she wasn't interested in it.

But before leaving us, the President [Roosevelt] looked for the mechanic, shook his hand, called him by name and thanked him for coming to Washington. And there was nothing **perfunctory** about his thanks. He meant what he said. I could feel that.[273]

An annual Division of Insurance competition hearing that had been so **perfunctory** in the past that the commissioner once skipped it, yesterday filled a Boston conference room to overflowing....[274]

write your own:

Pernicious

p&r-'ni-sh&s

(Adjective) harmful or destructive; deadly
Keyword: perm fishes (as in curling the "hair" on a fish)

Many people thought that Jane's idea to **perm fishes** was a cruel and **pernicious** thing to do.

The **pernicious** termites ate into the wooden foundation of the house, costing thousands of dollars in damage.

Radioactivity wasn't banned in consumer products until 1938. By this time it was much too late for Madame Curie, who died of leukemia in 1934. Radiation, in fact, is so **pernicious** and long lasting that even now her papers from the 1890s—even her cookbooks—are too dangerous to handle.[275]

Tragically, America's forests ... are being decimated at an alarming rate by large-scale catastrophic wildfire and massive outbreaks of disease and insect infestation. Each year, millions of acres of once-pristine forestland are ravaged by these **pernicious** wildland scourges.[276]

write your own:

Petulant

'pe-ch&-l&nt

(Adjective) bad tempered; rude or impatient; irritable

Keyword: pet for rent

The **petulant pet for rent** bared its teeth and growled before chewing up the man's leg.

The customer's **petulant** behavior was rude and difficult to deal with.

She was being what my father called "petulant," as in, "Susie, don't speak to me in that **petulant** tone."[275]

Most parents shake their heads and blame hormones when their teenager storms off and slams the door. But new research suggests that such **petulant** behavior could actually be due to normal brain "remodeling" that occurs during adolescence.[276]

write your own:

Philanthropic

"fi-l&n-'thrä-pik

(Adjective) being charitable or generous
Keyword: Phil in the tropics

Phil in the Tropics was a **philanthropic** hero, providing generous help to anyone in need.

The **philanthropic** businessman used his wealth to help the poor in his community.

His strong views on these subjects clearly influenced his five children. Assorted do-gooders, they're all involved in their father's **philanthropic** endeavors.[277]

Al Green ... was recently appointed to the Order of Canada in recognition of life-long **philanthropic** activities.[278]

write your own:

Phlegmatic

fleg-'ma-tik

(Adjective) unemotional; sluggish; dull
Keyword: flag mat

Because they felt it was not right to step on a flag mat, the **phlegmatic** employees worked especially slow to fill their orders for **flag mats**.

The **phlegmatic** psychologist had the ideal personality for his job because he had no trouble keeping emotional distance from his clients.

[He] was a **phlegmatic** man, a college graduate ... with an easy manner that the [Chicago's baseball team] Cubs interpreted as a lack of spirit.[279]

One realized the red-hot energy which underlay [Sherlock] Holmes's **phlegmatic** exterior when one saw the sudden change which came over him from the moment that he entered the fatal apartment. In an instant he was tense and alert....[280]

write your own:

Pique

'pEk

(Noun) resentment at being slighted; a feeling of hurt pride
(Verb) to provoke intrigue or interest
Keyword: peak

Tom was **piqued** at Jim who erroneously took all the credit in the news for reaching the **peak** of the mountain first.

The biggest thing damaged in the motorcycle accident was David's pride, but his **pique** quickly disappeared when he realized how lucky he was to be uninjured.

The story goes that the mural was made hurriedly, in a fit of **pique** after an argument....[279]

On the other hand, children who are truly loved, although in moments of **pique** they may consciously feel or proclaim that they are being neglected, unconsciously know themselves to be valued.[280]

write your own:

Placate

'plA-"kAt or 'pla-"kAt

(Verb) to soothe; to prevent anger
Keyword: play cake

To **placate** her father after he returned home grumpy from a hard day's work, the little girl gave him a **play cake** of rocks and dirt.

The shop owner attempted to **placate** his angry workers with higher wages and better benefits.

Since the last court date, in late June, [the company] and its lawyers had been involved in negotiations to **placate** those who appear to oppose the reorganization plan.[281]

If Stockings to Stuf runs out of a product, Weiner relies on his staff to **placate** the customer and make the sale.[282]

write your own:

Polemic

p&-'le-mik

(Noun) an attack or defense regarding a set of principles, ideals, or opinions; argument; debate; controversy

Note: A polemicist is an aggressive controversialist

Keyword: pole limit

The fisherman engaged in a **polemic** with the park warden, arguing that he was unhappy with the new **pole limit** of one fishing pole per family.

The televised **polemic** uncovered many scandals that the governor's administration had desperately been trying to conceal.

History is the **polemics** of the victor. -William F. Buckley, Jr.[285]

Shortly before his death he "lashed out at his critics in a **polemic** ... that charged them with perpetuating [carrying on] myths...."[286]

write your own: _____

Ponderous

'pän-d&-r&s or 'pän-dr&s

(Adjective) heavy or weighty/ slow or awkward because something is heavy or large/ boring or unpleasantly dull

Keyword: pond

His steps seemed **ponderous** as he struggled to move the heavy and awkward **pond**.

The teacher's slow and **ponderous** delivery made the lecture even more monotonous.

Ian Forrest succeeds in adapting Lewis Carroll's sometimes **ponderous** prose into a magical theatrical evening at the Theatre by the Lake.[283]

In a faster-moving world, this **ponderous** linear activity [of management] breaks down. It is too slow. It is not well enough informed with real-time information.[284]

write your own:

Precipitous

pri-'si-p&-t&s

(Adjective) very steep
Keyword: pressed lips

Several pairs of **pressed lips** smashed against the front window of the bus as it descended the **precipitous** mountain road.

Due to high interest rates and job layoffs, there was a **precipitous** fall in the sale of houses.

With the deep cuts [in jobs] came a **precipitous** drop in the airline's once-enviable customer service ratings. Complaints about Delta suddenly skyrocketed—everything from dirty planes and late departures to missing baggage.[289]

Entering last night's contest against Indiana, a 102-72 Celtics' loss, there had been a **precipitous** dip in Boston's 3-point shooting percentage over the last two games.[290]

write your own:

Precocious

pri-'kO-sh&s

(Adjective) prematurely advanced, especially in children
Keyword: free coaches

The **precocious** young chess player was given **free coaches** when he began training for the world championship.

Justin's teachers decided the **precocious** child was so smart she could skip the next two grades.

A sickly, **precocious** child, [French physicist, mathematician and theologian Blaise Pascal] had been closeted from other children and educated by his scientist father, who discovered that the eleven-year-old Blaise had secretly worked out for himself the first twenty-three propositions [math proofs] of Euclid ["father" of Geometry].[285]

Precocious and prolific, Hargrove was 20 when he cut his first record as a leader, won the Down Beat Readers' Poll ... and captured a Grammy last year....[286]

write your own:

Predilection

"pre-d&l-'ek-sh&n or "prE-d&l-'ek-sh&n

(Noun) a preconceived liking; a preference for something
Keyword: election

California voters seem to have a **predilection** for movie star candidates up for **election**-- voting several into office.

Danielle took a **predilection** to swimming when she was a child, and now she works every summer as a lifeguard.

The movie isn't as clever by half as Herrington's previous "A Murder of Crows," which pitted lawyer Cuba Gooding Jr. against a villain with a penchant [strong liking] for disguise and a **predilection** for literature.[291]

He was also a direct male-line descendant of Genghis Khan, though intervening generations and racial mixing had so juggled his genes that he had no discernible Mongoloid characteristics, and the only vestiges left in Mr. L. Prosser of his mighty ancestry were a pronounced stoutness about the turn and a **predilection** for little fur hats.[292]

write your own:

Pretentious

pri-'tent-sh&s or pri-'ten-sh&s

(Adjective) claiming or giving the appearance of unjustified importance or distinction

Keyword: pretend

George acted **pretentious** when he **pretended** to be a war hero, but in reality he was a coward.

Movie critics are often viewed as a **pretentious** group because their opinions are often presented as facts.

Orchids may seem to be the **pretentious**, stunning and oh-so-demanding supermodels of the flower world. But it's not so, say enthusiasts.[287]

They complain that the director of [the movie] Ocean's Eleven is being **pretentious** by working fast and cheap.[288]

write your own:

Proclivity

prO-'kli-v&-tE

(Noun) a tendency or inclination towards a particular thing
Keyword: no activity

Taylor had a **proclivity** for **no activity**, sleeping his life away.

Nancy's **proclivity** for drinking and pool playing is not acceptable to many of the people in her small town.

Working 16-hour days, six or seven days a week, he has put his concern for his patients above his personal life. Slightly rumpled, with a **proclivity** for bow ties, he yawns a lot.[291]

They are now faced with an extremely disillusioned [disappointed] investor base that shows no **proclivity** to become enlightened [informed] anytime soon.[292]

write your own:

Prodigious

(Adjective) enormous or extraordinary
Keyword: ditches

In his search for dinosaur bones, the little boy dug several **prodigious ditches**.

She lifted a **prodigious** amount of weight to free the trapped baby from beneath the derailed train.

She founded the nonprofit Ford's Theatre Society, became a **prodigious** fundraiser for the theater's original plays and musicals and produced more than 150 of them herself.[295]

At fifteen he was already winning the Academie Francaise's approving attention for his poems. He was nineteen when his mother died in 1821 and his boyhood experiences would color his whole **prodigious** output of novels, poetry and plays.[296]

write your own:

Profusion

pr&-'fyü-zh&n or prO-'fyü-zh&n

(Noun) large amount/ extravagance
Keyword: more fuse on

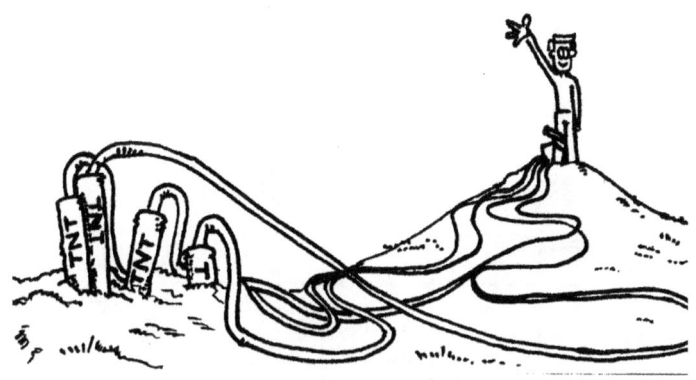

Afraid that the dynamite would explode too quickly, he put **more fuse on**, creating a **profusion** of fuse line.

The Girl Scouts sold such a **profusion** of Girl Scout cookies that it took them two weeks to deliver them.

Among a **profusion** of tips about how to choose from a restaurant menu and entertaining at home, her book supplies abundant advice on returning to the dieter's path, based on hard-won experience.[293]

At one time, the grass on the Boston Common [one of the oldest public parks in the USA] could hardly be seen for the **profusion** of woolly backs of sheep.[294]

write your own: _____

Section 8 Crossword Puzzle

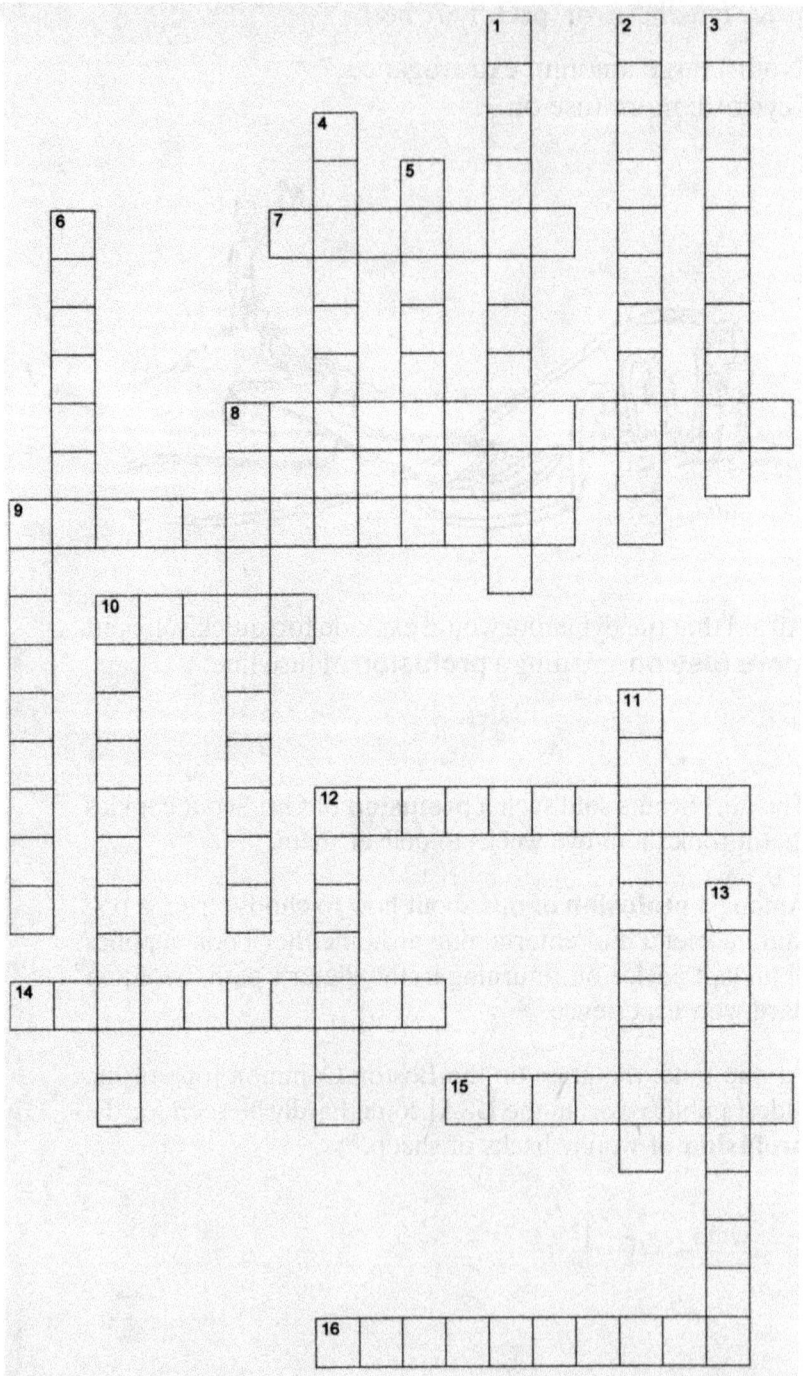

Across

7. an attack or defense regarding a set of principles, ideals, or opinions; argument; debate; controversy
8. being charitable or generous
9. a traveling about
10. resentment at being slighted; a feeling of hurt pride/ to provoke interest
12. prematurely advanced, especially in children
14. a tendency or inclination towards a particular thing
15. transparent; clear
16. harmful or destructive; deadly

Down

1. a preconceived liking; a preference for something
2. very steep
3. unemotional; sluggish; dull
4. large amount/ extravagance
5. bad tempered; rude or impatient; irritable
6. to soothe; to prevent anger
8. performed without care or interest/ done automatically
9. slow or awkward because something is heavy or large/ boring or unpleasantly dull
10. claiming or giving the appearance of unjustified importance or distinction
11. enormous or extraordinary
12. scarcity or lack of number
13. treacherous; not trustworthy

Section 8 Multiple Choice Review

Select the word that best fits each sentence.

1. His book never reached the best-seller list due to his _____ writing style.
   a. precocious   b. precipitous   c. ponderous   d. pretentious

2. The newspaper article angered him so much; it took a long time to finally _____ him.
   a. pique   b. placate   c. profuse   d. peregrinate

3. In her _____ she argued her cased and stated that she would stand by the cause no matter what happened.
   a. polemic   b. peregrination   c. predilection   d. proclivity

4. Tanner was _____ at the derisive criticism from the class, and consequently he harbored a grudge towards many of his classmates.
   a. profused   b. piqued   c. placated   d. peregrinated

5. Although the _____ new college graduate seemed inexperienced, his skills and expertise were very advanced despite his young age.
   a. prodigious   b. ponderous   c. pretentious   d. precocious

6. Matt loves the difficult black diamond ski routes—the more _____ the ski route the better.
   a. pretentious   b. prodigious   c. precipitous   d. pernicious

7. The _____ of selections in the fifty page lunch menu was overwhelming, making it very difficult for most people to order.
   a. paucity   b. predilection   c. proclivity   d. profusion

8. Wyatt acquired a(n) _____ for Mexican food after he spent the summer in Mexico City, and now orders it every chance he gets.
   a. polemic   b. profusion   c. petulant   d. predilection

9. As a result of his _____ for criminal behavior he was continuously sentenced to jail.
   a. paucity   b. perfunctory   c. proclivity   d. profusion

10. Instead of healing her injury, the iodine the nurse used had a(n) _____ effect and made the cut worse.
    a. perfidious   b. precipitous   c. precocious   d. pernicious

11. For the sunny afternoon, we decided to _____ down to the park to have a picnic.
    a. profuse   b. pique   c. peregrinate   d. placate

12. In many third world countries there is a _____ of school supplies. Paper and pencils are luxury items that cannot be afforded.
    a. pique   b. paucity   c. perfunctory   d. prodigious

13. His _____ feat of climbing the seven highest mountains in the fastest time was honored with a Guinness World Record.
    a. philanthropic   b. phlegmatic   c. polemic   d. prodigious

14. The _____ young lady felt she knew more about art then her professor.
    a. pretentious   b. philanthropic   c. ponderous   d. phlegmatic

15. The _____ dog had to be put outside for the day because he was behaving so badly.
    a. precocious   b. phlegmatic   c. pellucid   d. petulant

16. He donated two years of his time to the _____ organization to help less fortunate people.
    a. philanthropic   b. phlegmatic   c. perfidious   d. petulant

17. Mike's weekly chores became so _____ he could perform them quickly with his eyes closed.
    a. pellucid   b. polemic   c. perfunctory   d. petulant

18. The children could easily see several fish in the _____ lake because it was crystal clear.
    a. pellucid   b. ponderous   c. precipitous   d. petulant

19. Compared to her excitable twin sister, Rosa's _____ personality is surprising to most people.
    a. perfidious   b. pernicious   c. pretentious   d. phlegmatic

20. The bank robber had to dispose of all his _____ connections because he did not want to get caught.
    a. philanthropic   b. ponderous   c. perfidious   d. perfunctory

Section 8 Matching Review

Match the word on the left to the correct meaning on the right.

1. _____ Paucity
2. _____ Pellucid
3. _____ Peregrinate
4. _____ Perfidious
5. _____ Perfunctory
6. _____ Pernicious
7. _____ Philanthropic
8. _____ Petulant
9. _____ Phlegmatic
10. _____ Pique
11. _____ Placate
12. _____ Polemicist
13. _____ Ponderous
14. _____ Precipitous
15. _____ Precocious
16. _____ Predilection
17. _____ Prententious
18. _____ Proclivity
19. _____ Prodigious
20. _____ Profusion

A. performed without care or interest/ done automatically
B. slow or awkward because something is heavy or large/ boring or unpleasantly dull
C. scarcity or lack of number
D. unemotional; sluggish; dull
E. large amount/ extravagance
F. an aggressive controversialist
G. harmful or destructive; deadly
H. prematurely advanced, especially in children
I. to wander or travel from place to place
J. enormous or extraordinary
K. treacherous; not trustworthy
L. resentment at being slighted; a feeling of hurt pride/ to provoke interest
M. being charitable or generous
N. very steep
O. claiming or giving the appearance of unjustified importance or distinction
P. transparent; clear
Q. a tendency or inclination towards a particular thing
R. a preconceived liking; a preference for something
S. to soothe; to prevent anger
T. bad tempered; rude or impatient; irritable

Section Nine

Prolific

pr&-'li-fik

(Adjective) productive/ generating a large quantity of something

Note: Proliferate is a verb meaning to increase in number

Keyword: pro lifter

The **pro lifter** was very **prolific** with over a dozen children.

Theodore Roosevelt and Winston Churchill were two world leaders who were also **prolific** writers, producing dozens of books each.

His current working theory is that an extremely **prolific** female seeded the highly volcanic region with eggs over a period of decades, and the hatched young are reaching young adulthood....[297]

Born and raised in China, where his father was a missionary ... he received the Bronze Star ... and was also a **prolific** playwright [person who writes plays] and the author of a number of treatises on physics.[298]

write your own:

Prosaic

prO-'zA-ik

(Adjective) dull or lacking interest; ordinary
Keyword: mosaic

The new **mosaic** display at the art museum was **prosaic**, generating little interest because it was so dull and ordinary.

The **prosaic** handbook for Greg's new job put him to sleep every time he read it.

This book exposes all this in the calm, sometimes **prosaic** writing one would expect from an accountant....[301]

[Wagner] began using magnetic-resonance-imaging (MRI) machines and electron microscopes as cameras, magnifying or looking inside objects as **prosaic** as corncobs and as elusive [evanescent] as dividing cells.[302]

write your own:

Protract

prO-'trakt or pr&-'trakt

(Verb) to prolong or extend
Keyword: protractor

The kids moaned with despair as they believed that using **protractors** in math would **protract** the class period into their recess.

Brian **protracted** the romantic date with his girlfriend by offering to take her out for ice cream after the concert.

Tuck your chin so your head is in line with your body, and pull your toes toward your shins. **Protract** your shoulder blades while keeping your belly button drawn in.[299]

As to your expectations of a favorable answer from the Onondagas [Native American tribe], we must desire you to cut off your hope, and not **protract** it to any farther length; for we know by experience that hope deferred is very painful.[300]

write your own:

Provocation

"prä-v&-'kA-sh&n

(Noun) something that provokes one to anger or action
Keyword: lava formation

Mt. Saint Helen's eruption and rising **lava formation** was a **provocation** for locals and tourists to immediately flee the area.

After a week of **provocation** to join the church softball team by his pastor, Jim finally consented.

Disproportionate [out of proportion] rage or anger, overreaction to minor **provocation**, and cynicism are other embodiments [examples] of suppressed [bottled up] emotion.[303]

[He] called Barney "the most compelling, richly imaginative artist to emerge in years," and the exhibition "an inspired benchmark of ambition, scope and forthright **provocation** for art in the new century."[304]

write your own:

Pundit

'p&n-d&t

(Noun) a person who is an authority on a subject; of great learning/ a critic

Keyword: nun kit

The new nuns were excited after a religious **pundit** created **nun kits** for their training.

Nick was known as the trading card **pundit** in my class. He knew the exact value of all of his cards and all of the major league players' statistics.

To sell their books, tapes, and seminars, these **pundits** promised the masses a solution to their dilemma.[303]

Pundits can talk and talk and talk, using this piece of data and that bit of evidence to assure the American public that this is all going to play out in our favor.[304]

write your own:

Purport

'p&r-"pOrt or 'p&r-"port

(Verb) to profess or claim to be (often something you are not)
Keyword: fur port

The French had several **fur ports** along the Mississippi River, and they **purported** to be the best hunters—although the Native Americans were arguably better.

The book **purported** that anyone can get the best bargain by following three easy rules.

The survey—something less than scientific, since its results are based on reader votes—**purports** to show that the Midwest is emerging as a new area of artistic influence.[307]

From the time children are able even to grasp one of these wooden writing sticks [pencil], they use them to take an endless battery of tests that **purport** to measure their current ability and future potential.[308]

write your own: _____

Quixotic

kwik-'sä-tik

(Adjective) impractically idealistic
Keyword: quick sock fit

Looking for the **quick sock fit**, the **quixotic** prince asked every girl to try on the sock that was left behind at the palace sock hop.

The project was labeled **quixotic** by the committee, as it seemed too impractical and idealistic.

Begun as a **quixotic** gesture, blowpipes confronting bulldozers, the protests electrified the international environmental movement, leading then Senator Al Gore to describe the Penan as the frontline troops in the battle to save the Earth. But the logging continued.[311]

Some of the unexplained wealth was devoted to laudable [praiseworthy] public works—a modern road was built leading up to the village, for example, and facilities for running water were provided. Other expenditures were more **quixotic**. A tower was built, the Tour Magdala, overlooking the sheer side of the mountain. An opulent country house was constructed....[312]

write your own:

Raconteur

"ra-"kän-'t&r or "ra-"k&n-'t&r

(Noun) storyteller
Keyword: wreck on tour

The judge ordered the **raconteur** to take his **wreck on tour**. He had to drive his beat up car around the country, telling his story.

Around the campfire, the scoutmaster proved to be a brilliant **raconteur**, keeping the children spellbound with his stories.

One day in the waning years of his life, Red Pollard stopped talking. Perhaps it was a physical problem. Perhaps the old **raconteur** just didn't want to speak anymore.[307]

Rare as story talent is, we often meet people who seem to have it by nature, those street-corner **raconteurs** for whom storytelling is as easy as a smile.[308]

write your own: _____

Ramify

'ra-m&-"fI

(Verb) to divide or branch out
Keyword: rams

The **rams** forged new trails in the mountains, **ramifying** the existing former path into several branches.

The tourists were bewildered when the freeway seemed to **ramify** into several different roads at once.

For the next fifty years the park would remain "the great focus of travel, from which speedy communications will **ramify** in all directions."[309]

Mushrooms differ from plants in several ways. The part we eat is only one small portion of the organism, most of which lives invisibly underground as a fine, cottony network of fibers, or hyphae, which **ramify** through the soil to gather nutrients.[310]

write your own:

Raucous

'ro-k&s

(Adjective) rough-sounding/ in a disorderly and rowdy manner
Keyword: rock

Mike made a **raucous** noise that woke the neighbors by throwing **rocks** against his friend's window at night.

The room turned **raucous** within minutes after the rowdy kids arrived for the birthday party.

[Galveston] gained a reputation as a **raucous** hub of illicit gambling and wide-open sin until the mid-1950s, when Texas Rangers shut it down and indirectly helped to reinvent the city as a tourist destination and family resort.[313]

The 25th annual carnival parade was a **raucous** tribute to Latin culture....[314]

write your own: _____

Reprobate

're-pr&-"bAt

(Noun) an immoral, vicious person
Keyword: wreck a date

The **reprobate** was so mean and self-centered that he often **wrecked a date** with one mean comment.

Garrett was labeled a **reprobate** after he was caught beating a bunny.

I practically live on the Internet. Are my life and finances an open book for every intelligent **reprobate** who has a browser?[323]

After several waiting patients averted [turned away] their eyes, he realized he must look like a **reprobate**. He hadn't shaved during their trip and had spent a virtually sleepless night on the train.[324]

write your own:

Reticent

're-t&-s&nt

(Adjective) uncommunicative; tending to be silent; keeping to oneself
Keyword: rent a tent

Greg liked to keep to himself and decided that in order to remain **reticent** it would be best to **rent a tent** instead of staying in a cabin with his friends.

In police custody, he remained **reticent**, refusing to answer any questions about his whereabouts the previous evening.

But Burris, who isn't the least bit **reticent** to tell the world he isn't happy that the [Green Bay] Packers gave up on him after one season, won't hold back when it comes to providing the Bears staff any tidbit of information that might be used against his former team.[329]

His **reticent** manner was considered ideal for coping with the demands of celebrityhood.[330]

write your own:

Retrograde

're-tr&-"grAd

(Adjective) having a backward motion or direction

Keyword: grade

Instead of helping the student's **grades**, the tutor had a **retrograde** effect on the child's school work.

Though Tommy was an exceptional student, his mother did not want him to skip ahead a grade, fearing that it would create a **retrograde** effect on his social life.

But the trauma to her brain caused **retrograde** amnesia, erasing virtually her entire memory of the previous 18 months—including any recollection of the man she had fallen in love with and married.[323]

[Meriwether] Lewis hated to turn around. "This is the first time since we have been on this long tour that we have ever been compelled to retreat or make a **retrograde** march.--Lewis and Clark Expedition"[324]

write your own:

Ribald

'ri-b&ld, 'ri-bold, or 'rI-"bold

(Adjective) characterized by crude or indecent joking; vulgar
Keyword: real bald

The kids loved to tell **ribald** jokes about the man's **really bald** head.

William had a tendency to tell **ribald** jokes at church, and was consequently avoided.

In New Jersey, for example, when a drunken Republican editor was charged with making a **ribald** reference to the president's posterior [buttocks], the jury returned a not guilty verdict on the grounds that truth was a legitimate defense.[325]

Blonde, with intense, staring eyes, she could be disorienting silent in company and then, after a few drinks, **ribald**, witty, and by all accounts irresistible.[326]

write your own: _____

http://SolidA.net

Sagacity

s&-'ga-s&-tE or si-'ga-s&-tE

(Noun) good judgment; wisdom
Keyword: Sack City

Due to the **sagacity** of its leaders, sacks were recycled over and over again in **Sack City**.

Wendy was voted president of the student council due to her **sagacity** and good judgment on tough issues.

Showing measured restraint, skill with young talent and strong storytelling sense ... [he] brings **sagacity** and sympathy to "Antwone Fisher," a fictionalized drama....[327]

While man has sometimes succeeded in dragging the dog down to his level, the dog has only occasionally succeeded in raising man to his level of **sagacity**. –James Thurber[328]

write your own:

Salient

'sA-ly&nt or 'sA-lE-&nt

(Adjective) highly noticeable, prominent, or most important
Keyword: sail ants

The **sail ants** were highly **salient** as they sailed their little boat across the bathtub.

Journalism students are required to listen to speeches for the most important information, and then to report the most **salient** points.

Over the course of the last 25 years, Gallup researchers have qualitatively and quantitatively assessed the most **salient** employee perceptions [views] of management practices. Gallup researchers have sought to define a core set of statements that measure important perceptions across a wide spectrum of organizations.[333]

Cell phones won't display the same image as a PC; instead, information will be automatically scaled to best fit each display, preserving the **salient** details.[334]

write your own: _____

Salutary

'sal-y&-"ter-E

(Adjective) beneficial; improving
Keyword: salute

It is very **salutary** to **salute** the colonel in order to show respect for command and to avoid punishment.

Flunking the pretest was a **salutary** reminder that he needed to study more.

Wachtler's compassion for the other prisoners and his newly reconsidered ideas about the injustices of our legal system almost make one think it might be **salutary** for other judges to do a little hard time....[329]

Among other things, [Florence] Nightingale taught the British army about the **salutary** effects of sunlight, pure water, and clean kitchens. In two and a half years, the mortality rate among troops in England was cut in half.[330]

write your own:

Sanctimonious

"sa[ng]k-t&-'mO-nE-&s

(Adjective) acting morally superior; hypocritically pious or devout
 Keyword: sank

After his **sanctimonious** comment, "Nothing can sink us," the Titanic **sank**.

The boy's mother was **sanctimonious** around the other parents because she was president of the Parent-Teacher Organization and grand prize winner at the fair's bake-off competition.

He was intellectual but practical, spiritual but not **sanctimonious**, proud but never arrogant.[335]

Now, I [famous actor Sidney Poitier] couldn't tell him at the time, and maybe it'll sound a little **sanctimonious** even now, after all these years, but I rejected that part because, in my view, the character simply didn't measure up.[336]

write your own:

Sanguine

'sa[ng]-gw&n

(Adjective) cheerful, confident or optimistic
Keyword: penguin

The **sanguine penguin** was the biggest attraction at the zoo because he seemed so cheerful and upbeat.

Trying not to get his hopes up, Oscar was still secretly **sanguine**, feeling he had an excellent chance of getting the job promotion.

Arnold's former police chief … was **sanguine** this week as he discussed his chances of being reinstated [put back on the police force].[331]

[Former Olympic medalist Jenny] Thompson wasn't as **sanguine** as she seemed. Watching the [Olympic] individual events go off was agony.[332]

write your own:

Seminal

'se-m&-n&l

(Adjective) origin, or the beginning of something (often influencing later developments)
Keyword: cement ball

Some say the **seminal** beginning to the modern game of basketball originated with the Aztecs who played a similar game with a hard rubber ball that felt rather like a **cement ball**.

The **seminal** game "Pong," regarded by many as the first video game, may be credited for starting a new genre in entertainment.

[His] **seminal** work has made him a contender ... for a Nobel Prize.[339]

He played trombone and guitar with his brothers and cousins before hitting the road and embarking [starting] on a career that would lead him to such **seminal** jazz groups as the Count Basie Orchestra and the Bennie Moten band.[340]

write your own: _____

Section 9 Crossword Puzzle

Across

2. productive/ to generate a large quantity of something
4. cheerful, confident or optimistic
9. impractically idealistic
11. a person who is an authority on a subject; of great learning/ a critic
12. beneficial; improving
14. rough-sounding/ in a disorderly and rowdy manner
16. something that provokes one to anger or action
17. to profess or claim to be (often something you are not)

Down

1. origin; the beginning of something (often influencing later developments)
3. acting morally superior; hypocritically pious or devout
5. good judgment; wisdom
6. highly noticeable, prominent, or most important
7. characterized by crude or indecent joking; vulgar
8. to prolong or extend
10. uncommunicative; tending to be silent; keeping to oneself
13. storyteller
14. having a backward motion or direction
15. an immoral, vicious person
16. dull or lacking interest; ordinary
18. to divide or branch out

Section 9 Multiple Choice Review

Select the word that best fits each sentence.

1. The life of the automobile was _____ by taking it in for regular oil changes and for scheduled service maintenance.
   a. prolific   b. purported   c. protracted   d. ramified

2. Ignoring his antagonist's _____, Victor turned around and walked away from him.
   a. sagacity   b. raucous   c. prosaic   d. provocation

3. Erin acted _____ around her colleagues after receiving the academic scholarship.
   a. salient   b. sanctimonious   c. quixotic   d. reticent

4. The teenage _____ was considered both mean and immoral, and appeared to be on a fast track to prison.
   a. raconteur   b. retrograde   c. provocation   d. reprobate

5. Charlie did not want to talk about his past and remained _____.
   a. reticent   b. sanguine   c. prosaic   d. sanctimonious

6. Though computers allow for more free and constant communication, some may argue that it is less personal, and therefore a _____ step in human interaction.
   a. retrograde   b. salutary   c. prosaic   d. sanguine

7. The film-maker attributed his success to his skill as a _____, with a natural ability for weaving a good tale.
   a. reprobate   b. raconteur   c. pundit   d. provocation

8. Knowing his defense was not too strong; the lawyer skirted the _____ facts of the case and attempted to focus on smaller details.
   a. prolific   b. seminal   c. salient   d. seminal

9. The _____ experience of the near drowning in the pool left all the life guards more cautious and alert.
   a. salutary   b. salient   c. protracted   d. sagacious

10. The applicant's _____ character made him unfit, in the eyes of the school, to work with children.
    a. sanguine   b. salutary   c. ribald   d. sanctimonious

11. Vicky was _____ about finally being released from the hospital and began to plan what she wanted to do when she arrived home.
    a. reticent   b. sanguine   c. sagacious   d. ribald

12. As the first scientist to study the topic, Dr. Tony Smith was especially pleased to see his _____ work published.
    a. purported   b. quixotic   c. retrograde   d. seminal

13. It's hard to get an appointment with my hair stylist if you are not a regular customer, as she is considered a cosmetology _____.
    a. pundit   b. reprobate   c. raconteur   d. ribald

14. His troubles _____ as his lie branched out into a series of problems.
    a. reprobated   b. retrograded   c. ramified   d. purported

15. The _____ politician always considered what he was going to say before speaking in order to portray his ideas correctly.
    a. sanguine   b. salient   c. ribald   d. sagacious

16. Susan's book centers on a(n) _____ character who finds the meaning of life in chivalry. He tries to come to the rescue of nearly anyone, even if it is well beyond his ability or means.
    a. quixotic   b. raucous   c. pundit   d. ramified

17. Michael Jordan is one of the most _____ scorers in NBA history.
    a. quixotic   b. prolific   c. protracted   d. raucous

18. The liquid vitamin drink was _____ to contain all of the necessary vitamins the body needs and in the exact proportions.
    a. protracted   b. purported   c. quixotic   d. proliferated

19. The talent show was _____ and failed to hold our interest.
    a. seminal   b. reticent   c. prolific   d. prosaic

20. Due to his _____ voice, people who first meet Chris tend to believe that he is a tough character, but in actuality he is very gentle.
    a. pundit   b. raconteur   c. purported   d. raucous

Section 9 Matching Review

Match the word on the left to the correct meaning on the right.

1. ____ Prolific/Proliferate
2. ____ Prosaic
3. ____ Protract
4. ____ Provocation
5. ____ Pundit
6. ____ Purport
7. ____ Quixotic
8. ____ Raconteur
9. ____ Ramify
10. ____ Raucous
11. ____ Reprobate
12. ____ Reticent
13. ____ Retrograde
14. ____ Ribald
15. ____ Sagacity
16. ____ Salient
17. ____ Salutary
18. ____ Sanctimonious
19. ____ Sanguine
20. ____ Seminal

A. characterized by crude or indecent joking; vulgar
B. having a backward motion or direction
C. to profess or claim to be (often something you are not)
D. a person who is an authority on a subject; of great learning/ a critic
E. something that provokes one to anger or action
F. dull or lacking interest; ordinary
G. productive/ to generate a large quantity of something
H. beneficial; improving
I. origin; the beginning of something (often influencing later developments)
J. acting morally superior; hypocritically pious or devout
K. highly noticeable, prominent, or most important
L. impractically idealistic
M. storyteller
N. to prolong or extend
O. uncommunicative; tending to be silent; keeping to oneself
P. to divide or branch out
Q. rough-sounding/ in a disorderly and rowdy manner
R. an immoral, vicious person
S. cheerful, confident or optimistic
T. good judgment; wisdom

Section Ten

Sequester

si-'kwes-t&r

(Verb) to remove or set apart/
to put into isolation
Keyword: pester

Because Cecilia was **pestering** her little brother, her mother **sequestered** her to her bedroom for the afternoon.

At the airport, the customs officials **sequestered** illegal animal products entering the country.

In the 19th century, the rich began to **sequester** themselves in neighborhoods from Gramercy Park in New York to the Central West End in St. Louis.[341]

Attorneys for [the] sniper suspect ... are asking a Fairfax County judge to appoint five criminal investigators to help them prepare for his capital murder trial and may seek to **sequester** the jury....[342]

write your own:

Serendipity

"ser-&n-'di-p&-tE

(Noun) a pleasant, accidental discovery
Keyword: Seven dips

It was a case of **serendipity** when the chef accidentally tripped and spilled his **seven dips** together which resulted in his world famous chip dip.

In 1928, Alexander Fleming made the **serendipitous** discovery of penicillin when he noticed that a culture plate containing bacteria was contaminated by mold.

In a classic example of **serendipity**, a survey originally designed to improve the way astronomers estimate the distance to elliptical galaxies has now revealed large-scale bulk motions among the galaxies.[343]

Whether or not it was **serendipity**, the initial sighting of Chang [later to become a world class tennis player] came at an indoor tennis club ... The pint-size youngster was running through drills with his older brother....[344]

write your own:

http://SolidA.net   ©Solid A, Inc.   253

Sophistry

'sä-f&-strE

(Noun) clever use of reasoning or argumentation that seems true but is false
Keyword: sofa history

The sellers used clever **sophistry** to sell the sofa, making up an elaborate story about the **sofa's history**.

Until the true facts were uncovered, his **sophistry** fooled many people.

The **sophistry** of this argument fairly filled me with rage. I knew not how to counter such nonsense.[345]

When he was forty years of age, and after he had been a member of Congress, he studied Euclid so that he [Abraham Lincoln] could detect **sophistry** and demonstrate his conclusions. [346]

write your own:

Soporific

"sä-p&-'ri-fik

(Adjective) causing sleep or drowsiness
Keyword: Soap Terrific

Soap Terrific contains a **soporific** ingredient that tends to make people sleepy.

The slow, repetitive beat of the music had a **soporific** effect on the audience, causing many people to fall asleep.

Overstimulated folk used to be sent to relax in the **soporific** climate of Bournemouth [England].[347]

I think Reza believes our culture has made us all so numb with constant media bombardment that ordinary theatre has a **soporific** quality. I think you have to get right up in people's face and scream at them, if not vocally, with images.[348]

write your own:

Stymie

'stI-mE

(Verb) to hinder or obstruct; to check or block
Keyword: sty (pig pen)

The child's bedroom was such a pig **sty** that the clutter **stymied** his mother's attempt to enter the room to tuck him in at night.

Her older brother got in her way and **stymied** her attempt to get the last slice of cheesecake.

Inevitably such [company policy] manuals are collections of "don'ts." And "don'ts" stop initiative [ambition], squelch innovation [origin creations], **stymie** creativity.[351]

During week 2 ... you will also learn how to avoid some of the common pitfalls that can **stymie** your progress.[352]

write your own:

Superfluous

su-'p&r-flü-&s

(Adjective) extra; exceeding the necessary amount
Keyword: super floss

The government's **superfluous** spending on **super floss** for the Statue of Liberty was unnecessary.

The teacher crossed out the **superfluous** words in the students' essays to illustrate how to write more concisely.

I think my biggest strength, at least the strength that will have the biggest impact on our success, is my ability to see through fluffy, **superfluous** information and cut to the point that matters. I have a way of eliminating unnecessary details and getting to the heart of an issue....[359]

Which brings us to Cassandra Wilson. I mean Cassandra: Fame has rendered the last name **superfluous**....[360]

write your own: _____

Supersede

"sü-p&r-'sEd"

(Verb) to take the place of; to replace

Keyword: super seed

Note: also spelled "supercede"

Jack's **super seed** outgrew and **superseded** all of the beanstalks in the garden and reached up through the clouds.

Setting a new record in the men's 400 meter race, Jose **superceded** Samuel as the school's All Star Athlete.

My authority comes from the attorney general and **supercedes** that of your chief of police.[359]

At what point does an athlete's personal business become our business? When does a fan's right to know **supercede** the right to privacy?[360]

write your own:

Surreptitious

"s&r-&p-'ti-sh&s"

(Adjective) done in secret; hidden
Keyword: syrup dishes

When no one was looking, John **surreptitiously** allowed his dog to help wash the **syrup dishes** by licking them clean.

The teacher knew that Jimmy could hardly wait for recess when he noticed his **surreptitious** glance at the clock.

Her payload deposited, the lady scurries away to meet co-conspirator June—she doesn't want her full name revealed—at a white Volkswagen parked a block distant. Now it's June's turn to do the **surreptitious** feeding [of the pigeons]. [363]

In films, magazines, books, music and fashion imagery, the cigarette has become a standard fixture, emerging not from the **surreptitious** promotional efforts of tobacco multinationals but from a perception that "smoking is cool again."[364]

write your own:

Sycophant

'si-k&-f&nt or 'si-k&-"fant
(Noun) one who flatters without sincerity
Keyword: sick of ants

The roach was **sick of ants** living like **sycophants** in his motel—always flattering him but rarely paying.

The family accused the young bride of being a **sycophant**—full of flattery but really only interested in the millionaire's money.

When the family business is rock stardom, however, the perks —international adoration, untold wealth, glamorous **sycophants**—might make taking after dear old dad a tad more palatable [acceptable].[365]

The special interests and the **sycophants** will stand in the rain a week to see you and will treat you like a king. They'll come sliding in and tell you you're the greatest man alive....[366]

write your own:

Tawdry

'to-drE or 'tä-drE

(Adjective) cheap; showy in a tasteless way; gaudy
Keyword: tall tree

The Christmas ornaments on the **tall tree** looked rather **tawdry**, as if they were purchased at a five and dime store.

The actress's gown looked glamorous onscreen, however its sequins and gems looked plastic and **tawdry** up close.

The Group's focus on the urban underbelly [the city's corrupt area], and its emphasis on the life-styles of ordinary, working class Londoners in a run-down, **tawdry** area, had a resounding impact.[363]

Somewhere in Australia, an auto-sales company is using a **tawdry** Audrey Hepburn lookalike—in TV and print ads....[364]

write your own: _____

Temerity

t&-'mer-&-tE

(Noun) nerve; recklessness; boldness arising from contempt of danger or opposition

Keyword: to marry

With great **temerity** the boy decided **to marry** his girlfriend even though her mobster father vehemently opposed it.

Larry had the **temerity** to rebel against his teacher, even though he knew it could mean the loss of his recesses.

However, he could see that Mother was right: the king might believe, or pretend to believe, that no one could have the **temerity** to rebel against him....[365]

A criminal lawyer, Nouman had the **temerity** to defend a man Uday wanted punished for insulting his girlfriend, and Nouman paid for it with nearly two decades' worth of torment....[366]

write your own:

Tenacity

t&-'na-s&-tE

(Noun) extreme persistence or determination
Keyword: ten cities

Sean demonstrated great **tenacity**, running nonstop to **ten cities**.

With many hurdles to overcome and miles to endure, her **tenacity** helped her to win the triathlon.

Witt describes the heroism and the **tenacity** of Americans who survive the worst and recover against the greatest odds.[367]

And then there was Lee Iacocca, who had his back to the wall, painted into a corner and hanging by his fingernails, among other metaphoric travails—a regular industrial Indiana Jones. But he led Chrysler from the Temple of Doom, and his struggle demonstrated what can be achieved with talent and **tenacity**.[368]

write your own:

Transient

'tran-zE-&nt or 'tran-sh&nt

(Adjective) temporary or brief
Keyword: trance

Being hypnotized and put in a brief **transient trance** is a small price to pay for the possibility of a life long cure from tobacco addiction.

The **transient** storm blew through town, causing a great deal of damage in a short amount of time.

The city is building a marina for **transient** visiting boaters....[375]

Recorded in London with British musicians, it's a mature, assured song cycle that deals with the classic themes of the **transient** nature of love and existence.[376]

write your own:

Truncate

'tr&[ng]-"kAt or 'tr&n-"kAt

(Verb) to shorten
Keyword: trunk

The stewardess **truncated** the man's **trunk** with a saw so it would fit into the overheard compartment on the plane.

Americans often like to **truncate** the first names of people. Pamela is referred to as Pam. Patrick becomes Pat.

While many merchants already **truncate** the 16-digit card numbers on receipts, Visa will require, beginning July 1, that new credit-card machines display only the last four digits....[377]

The [computer] program can **truncate** the password at 8 characters, so those extra 192 characters never get written into memory anywhere.[378]

write your own:

http://SolidA.net ©Solid A, Inc.

Turpitude

't&r-p&-"tyüd

(Noun) wickedness; shamefulness; a corrupt act
Keyword: turnip dude

The **turnip dude** spent five months in jail for his acts of **turpitude** which included throwing rotten turnips through windows.

George could almost always be found engaging in some activity of moral **turpitude**, from copying assignments or tests to cheating at any competitive game on the playground.

Moral **turpitude** on Herbert's part was inconceivable [unthinkable]. Whatever he was up to, it had to be for a good cause.[379]

Cobb County public school officials will discuss a system-wide conduct code today that would suspend any athlete from the team who is charged with a felony or "misdemeanor involving moral **turpitude**."[380]

write your own:

Ungainly

"&n-'gAn-lE"

(Adjective) awkward or clumsy
Keyword: game

His **ungainly** manners during the **game** upset the other player.

The model's **ungainly** strut down the walkway seemed strangely unfitting and awkward.

Her mood was not improved by the baby she carried, which made her **ungainly** and nothing like the graceful lady of the house she felt herself to be.[377]

The only real complaint that can be leveled against the book's production is that the print is unjustified-that is, the lines do not all end at the same point on the page, which creates **ungainly** and irritating serration [uneven margin].[378]

write your own:

Vacillate

'va-s&-"lAt

(Verb) to fluctuate between opposing ideas; to waver

Keyword: Vaseline

With so many types of **Vaseline** available, he was unable to make up his mind and **vacillated** between his choices.

Kristi **vacillated** about whether or not to purchase the dress for weeks until it was no longer available.

We **vacillate** and fluctuate. How we feel about our decisions—even the way we make them—changes from day to day.[381]

She found herself starting to question, waiver, doubt, and **vacillate**.[382]

write your own:

Vapid

'va-p&d or 'vA-p&d

(Adjective) dull, uninteresting or lacking liveliness
Keyword: rapids

The usually exciting **rapids** in the river were calm, making what once was our vacation highlight, a **vapid** experience.

The audience became bored with the dull and **vapid** performance of the actors in the theater production.

You think he's **vapid**, dim-witted, with his stupidity arising....[385]

Lara Merriken was on a hike, gnawing on a **vapid** energy bar, when inspiration struck. "Why isn't somebody making something that is healthy, tastes good, and is made with wholly unprocessed foods?" she asked herself.[386]

write your own:

Voluble

'väl-y&-b&l

(Adjective) talking with ease
Keyword: volleyball

The **voluble volleyball** players ended up talking for hours instead of playing their game.

Nobody would have guessed that English was not the first language of the **voluble** guest. He was so fluent, and talked with such ease.

Acid freaks [drug addicts who take acid] are not given to **voluble** hospitality; they stare fixedly at strangers, or look right through them.[391]

Given half the chance, Brian Gaines, a **voluble** sort never short on ideas, will tell you he has many identities: new father, husband, Noe Valley neighbor, nonprofit executive director, friend.[392]

write your own:

Zealot

'ze-l&t

(Noun) a fanatic; a person who shows great enthusiasm for a cause
Keyword: sell it

Learn to be a sales **zealot** by reading the enthusiastic book, "You Name It, I Can **Sell It**."

Joan, a running **zealot**, refuses to take a day off, rain or shine.

Boston can be a rough place to play.... Slow starts are not forgiven. You have to perform or the local sports **zealots** jump all over you.[399]

She was a religious **zealot** who insisted he attend church services daily, and frequently accused him of sinful transgressions.[400]

write your own: _____

Section 10 Crossword Puzzle

Across

4. wickedness; shamefulness; a corrupt act
6. talking with ease
8. nerve; recklessness; boldness arising from contempt of danger or opposition
11. clever use of reasoning or argumentation that seems true but is false
14. to shorten
17. causing sleep or drowsiness
18. a pleasant, accidental discovery
19. awkward or clumsy

Down

1. cheap; showy in a tasteless way; gaudy
2. to take the place of; to replace
3. a fanatic; a person who shows great enthusiasm for a cause
5. temporary or brief
7. one who flatters without sincerity
9. to hinder or obstruct; to check or block
10. extra; exceeding the necessary amount
12. done in secret; hidden
13. to remove or set apart/ to put into isolation
14. extreme persistence or determination
15. dull, uninteresting or lacking liveliness
16. to fluctuate between opposing ideas; to waver

Section 10 Multiple Choice Review

Select the word that best fits each sentence.

1. When the prisoner acted up, he was _____ to the isolation cell for 48 hours.
   a. sequestered   b. stymied   c. vacillated   d. superseded

2. The mother was upset with the _____ happy meal toy and explained to her child that this was a cheap and worthless toy.
   a. soporific   b. surreptitious   c. tawdry   d. vapid

3. The new sign being built is to _____ the old, rusty one formerly used by the company.
   a. sequester   b. supersede   c. stymie   d. sequester

4. The skier's mistakes and _____ performance took him out of the final competition.
   a. ungainly   b. voluble   c. vacillated   d. superfluous

5. Computer networks were _____ after computer viruses overloaded servers with too much email.
   a. stymied   b. truncated   c. voluble   d. superseded

6. Lisa often told people that finding her husband was a true case of _____; they literally bumped into each other.
   a. serendipity   b. turpitude   c. sophistry   d. temerity

7. In the face of risking her job, she had the _____ to ask her boss for a raise.
   a. temerity   b. tenacity   c. sophistry   d. serendipity

8. Her mood _____ from one extreme to the other; one day she seems like the nicest person on the planet and the next she is grumpy and continually complaining.
   a. truncates   b. validates   c. vacillates   d. supersedes

9. The lawyer's _____ won him the case, but he later felt guilty about the erroneous statements he made to gain victory.
   a. temerity   b. sophistry   c. tawdry   d. tenacity

10. Though the student worked very hard on the painting, it looked _____ and bland.
    a. vapid   b. ungainly   c. soporific   d. voluble

11. Even though there was a rule about eating in the classroom, the teacher sneaked a _____ bite of a cookie when her students were not looking.
    a. transient   b. surreptitious   c. ungainly   d. tawdry

12. I always questioned Jerry's motives when he complemented me because I had been warned that he was a _____.
    a. zealot   b. transient   c. sycophant   d. vapid

13. Her thoughts of running away to Europe for a year were _____; there were so many other things she also wanted to do.
    a. voluble   b. superfluous   c. surreptitious   d. transient

14. The new calculator she purchased rounds or _____ numbers at the third decimal place.
    a. truncates   b. supersedes   c. stymies   d. vacillates

15. The _____ of his opponents made the game unfair, since his team followed all the rules.
    a. sophistry   b. turpitude   c. sycophant   d. zealot

16. The television station looked for a _____ person to fill the new position of the talk show host.
    a. transient   b. tawdry   c. surreptitious   d. voluble

17. The professor's _____ tone of voice during the slide show lulled a majority of the students to sleep.
    a. vapid   b. sequestered   c. superfluous   d. soporific

18. Four-year-old Dylan is always watching ants, impressed at their _____ and persistence in getting around any object he put in their way.
    a. temerity   b. serendipity   c. tenacity   d. sophistry

19. When hiking, I try to avoid packing _____ clothing in order to travel lightly.
    a. tawdry   b. vapid   c. superfluous   d. ungainly

20. Julie was a considered a _____ in her effort to raise money to preserve the rainforest.
    a. sycophant   b. vapid   c. transient   d. zealot

Section 10 Matching Review

Match the word on the left to the correct meaning on the right.

1. _____ Sequester
2. _____ Serendipity
3. _____ Sophistry
4. _____ Soporific
5. _____ Stymie
6. _____ Supersede
7. _____ Superfluous
8. _____ Surreptitious
9. _____ Sycophant
10. _____ Tawdry
11. _____ Temerity
12. _____ Tenacity
13. _____ Transient
14. _____ Truncate
15. _____ Turpitude
16. _____ Ungainly
17. _____ Vacillate
18. _____ Vapid
19. _____ Voluble
20. _____ Zealot

A. temporary or brief
B. extreme persistence or determination
C. a fanatic; a person who shows great enthusiasm for a cause
D. to take the place of; to replace
E. to hinder or obstruct; to check or block
F. nerve; recklessness; boldness arising from contempt of danger or opposition
G. done in secret; hidden
H. talking with ease
I. a pleasant, accidental discovery
J. to shorten
K. one who flatters without sincerity
L. clever use of reasoning or argumentation that seems true but is false
M. cheap; showy in a tasteless way; gaudy
N. to fluctuate between opposing ideas; to waver
O. awkward or clumsy
P. to remove or set apart/ to put into isolation
Q. dull, uninteresting or lacking liveliness
R. causing sleep or drowsiness
S. wickedness; shamefulness; a corrupt act
T. extra; exceeding the necessary amount

Free Resources

Free Resources @ www.solida.net

Audio Recordings

 Eliminate the worry of mispronouncing the words by listening to the online audio recordings .

Cartoon Animations

Watch select words from this book come to life in funny and memorable cartoon animations which are sure to make you smile.

Templates

Print or download the "Create Your Own" template to create your own VOCABBUSTERS for your own words.

Learning Style Assessment

Find out more about your learning or cognitive style by taking a free online assessment.

Vocabulary Resources

Discover other great free vocabulary and educational resources and links for teachers, parents and students which can also be accessed at this site.

Create Your Own

Word: _____

Defintion: _____

_____

_____

Caption: _____

_____

Example Sentence: _____

_____

_____

_____

For a free downlad of this template, go to www.solida.net

Example Sentence References

A. Parker, K. (4 December 2003). Cartoon harrumphers should loosen up. *The Witchita Eagle*, p. 11A.[A]
B. Martel, Y. (2001). *Life of Pi*. Orlando, F: Harcourt Books, Inc., p. 258.[B]

1. Stephan, A. (2003, March 6). It is now emerging that the Columbia space shuttle had serious problems on 20 of its 28 flights, and that a near-disaster in 1999 was hushed up. *New Statesman, 132*, 8.[1]
2. Adande, J.A. (2003, April 23). Lakers' Minnesota flats: No time to panic, but maybe that's the big problem. *Los Angeles Times*, Sports, p. 1.[2]
3. Lieberman, D. J. (1998). *Never Be Lied To Again: How to Get the Truth in 5 Minutes or Less in any Conversation or Situation*. New York: St. Martin's Press, p. 77.[3]
4. Walsh, K. T. & Whitelaw, K. (2003, January 20). The year of living dangerously. *U.S. News and World Report*, p. 16.[4]
5. Mitchard, J. (2000, April 30). Sad case, but not grounds for a legal case. *Milwaukee Journal Sentinel*. Retrieved December 22, 2003, from JSOnline http://www.jsonline.com/lifestyle/advice/apr00/mitccol30042900a.asp[5]
6. Kluger, R. (1992, March 30). The sheriff of Nottingham. *People Weekly, 37*, 34.[6]
7. Ward, M. (1998, June 15). The infinitely tiny neutrino may give physics big reality check *Milwaukee Journal Sentinel*. Retrieved December 22, 2003, from JSOnline, http://www.jsonline.com/archive/news/0615matters.stm[7]
8. Collins, Jr., L. (2001, November 25). Simplifying, relatively speaking. *The Houston Chronicle*, p. 19.[8]
9. Hernandez, N. (2003, May 15). "What an [expletive] thing to say"… to Ted Turner. *The Washington Post*, p. T02.[9]
10. Collins, Jim (2001). *Good to Great: Why Some Companies Make the Leap… and Others Don't*. HarperCollins Publishers: New York, NY, p.36.[10]
11. McLean, A. & Eldred, G. W. (2003). *Investing in Real Estate*. Hoboken, NJ: John Wiley and Sons, Inc., p. 253.[11]
12. Monroe, V. (June 2003). How to raise the men we'd want to marry. *O Magazine*, p. 163.[12]
13. Williams, K. (2002, November 28). Love of Doo Wop gave birth to a business. *The Washington Post*, p. T05.[13]
14. Cochrane, D. (2003, July). Master of many media: John Wilson reveals and interprets the inner selves of the people he portrays using brush, graphite, clay, and etching tools. *American Artist, 67*, 56.[14]
15. Valdmanis, T. (2003, March 5). Quattrone quits CSFB to focus on defense. *USA Today*, p. 2B.[15]
16. Stone, D. (2000). *Difficult Conversations: How to Discuss what Matters Most*. New York: Penguin Group, p. 39.[16]
17. Internet stuck in libel web. (2002, December 11). *Australian Financial Review*, p. 54.[17]
18. Bryson, Bill (2003). *A Short History of Nearly Everything*. Broadway Books: USA, p. 145.[18]
19. Newfield, J. (2003, March 17). How the other half still lives; in the shadow of wealth, New York's poor increase. *The Nation, 276*, 11.[19]
20. Meek, J. (2002, August 20). Magic of mushrooms gets medical nod. *The Guardian*, p.5.[20]
21. SerVaas, C. (1994, July-August). The Post investigates B12 deficiency. *Saturday Evening Post, 266*, 48-54.[21]
22. Castanon, R. (2003, May 25). Unhappy citizens have own lobbyist. *San Antonio Express-News*, p. 4H.[22]

23. Hare, J. (2002, December). Surviving the Sahara: hypnotic sands, freezing winds ... camels weak from hunger ... evil spirits and an explorer's shadow ... Not your normal winter getaway. *National Geographic, 202*, 54-78.[23]
24. Schutze, J. (2002, August 22). Crossing division street. How do white people learn what to think about race? It's best not to think about it. *Dallas Observer.* Retrieved December 18, 2003, from http://www.dallasobserver.com/issues/2002-08-22/feature.html/1/index.html.[24]
25. Nash, M. (2003, February 3). Cracking the ice: Antarctica is a vast, frozen mystery. Is it thawing, threatening coastal cities? Or is it, in fact, freezing? What scientists have learned. *Time, 161*, 50.[25]
26. Naudi, J. (2003, May 29). Building relationships. *St. Louis Post-Dispatch*, p. C1.[26]
27. Ambrose, S. (1996). *Undaunted Courage: Meriwether Lewis Thomas Jefferson and the Opening of the American West.* New York: Touchstone, p. 32.[27]
28. Isherwood, C. (2000, November 27). Kit Marlowe. *Variety, 381*, 29.[28]
29. Phillips, D. T. (1992). *Lincoln on Leadership: Executive Strategies for Tough Times.* New York: Warner Books, Inc., p. 138.[29]
30. Bing, S. (1997, February 3). Stepping up to the firing line. *Fortune, 135*, 51.[30]
31. For the record. (2002, December 17). *The Boston Globe*, p. C23.[31]
32. Covey, Stephen M.R., Merrill, Rebecca, and Covey, Stephen R. (2006). *The Speed of Trust: The One Thing that Changes Everything.* Free Press: New York, NY, p. 166. [32]
33. Rowley, H. (2001, November 19). London after Bloomsbury. *The Nation*, 273, 28.[33]
34. Budick, A. (2003, April 20). Hidden treasures of the Met. *Newsday*, p. 20.[34]
35. Davidson, A. (1999). *The Oxford Companion to Food.* New York: Oxford University Press. p. 389.[35]
36. Parshall, Jonathan and Tully Anthony (2005). *Shattered Sword: The Untold Story of the Battle of Midway,* p. 210. [36]
37. Elliott, C. (2003, June). Lagging behind? Get ahead of jet lag before it gets the best of you. *Entrepreneur, 31*, 24.[37]
38. Loewen, J. W. (1995). *Lies My Teacher Told Me: Everything Your American History Textbook Got Wrong.* New York: Simon and Schuster, Inc, p. 262.[38]
39. American Academy of Pediatrics (1991). *Caring for Your Baby and Young Child: Birth to Age 5.* New York: Bantam Books, p. 348.[39]
40. Melton, R. H. (2003, February 3). Businessman and politics aren't mixing in Richmond. *The Washington Post*, p. 01.[40]
41. Gourevitch, A. (2003, March). Better living through chemistry: DDT could save millions of Africans from dying of malaria—if only environmentalists would let it. *Washington Monthly, 35*, 19-24.[41]
42. Abrashoff, Micheal (2002). *It's Your Ship: Management Techniques from the Best Damn Ship in the Navy.* New York: Warner Books, Back Cover.[42]
43. Morton, A. (1998). *Diana: Her True Story in her Own Words.* New York: Simon and Schuster, Inc., Front Matter.[43]
44. England, T. (2003, June 8). E-Books rise slowed, but they're here. *The Santa Fe New Mexican.* Retrieved December 22, from the Santa Fe New Mexico database.[44]
45. Pollard, S. (2002, September 18). Saddam is more than welcome to George Galloway. *The Times* (London), p. 20.[45]
46. Moore, L.W. (1997, October 4). No contest: Corporate lawyers and the perversion of justice in America. *America, 177*, 33.[46]
47. Abrams, A. (2003, April). Depth in lights and darks: Cecile Baird creates dynamic colored-pencil and oil still lifes with a keen sense of palette and a devotion to light. *American Artist, 67*, 50-8.[47]
48. Akasie, J. (2000, February 21). Car Crazy. *Forbes. 165*, 54a.[48]
49. Dater, A. (2003, April 7). Avalanche 5, Blues 2 - Colorado clinches division title. *The Denver Post*, p.1.[49]

50. Reid, T. R. (2003, May). The Sherpas. *National Geographic*, p. 64.[50]
51. Milligan, S. (2002, July 25). The nation: House votes to expel Traficant: Ohio democrat is second ousted since Civil War. *The Boston Globe*, p. 2.[51]
52. Castle, T. (2002, October 14). Art with a proper stranger. *The New Republic, 227*, 28.[52]
53. Fort, T. (2003, March 1). Rites of spring. *The Times*, Features, p. 3.[53]
54. Gladwell, M. (2002). *The Tipping Point: How Little Things Can Make a Big Difference*. Little, USA: Brown and Company, p. 163.[54]
55. Belsky, G. (1999). *Why Smart People Make Big Money Mistakes and How To Correct Them: Lessons From The New Science Of Behavioral Economics*. New York: Fireside, p. 98.[55]
56. McManus, E. R. (2003). *Uprising: A Revolution of the Soul*. Nashville, TN: Thomas Nelson, Inc, p. 51.[56]
57. Anderson, D. (2003, May 12). Movies. Sydney Morning Herald, *The Guide*, p.14.[57]
58. Hendrick, B. (2003, April 4). War in the Gulf. Overview: Battle for Baghdad: "Forget the Rambo stuff." *The Atlanta Journal*-Constitution, p. 12A.[58]
59. Walker, C. (2003, May 26). Wreath-laying honors memory of the fallen; Iraq war lends gravity to salute to war dead. *The Baltimore Sun*, p. 2B.[59]
60. Logan, G. (2003, May 15). Rest for weary; Scott plans next round from TV chair. *Newsday*, p. A73.[60]
61. Bondy, F. (2003, March 27). Hughes on edge view from 6th another world. *Daily News*, p. 98.[61]
62. Crane, D. (2003, May 31). Soaring dollar makes Canada less competitive. *Toronto Star*, p. C02.[62]
63. Johnson, C. (2004). *The Sorrows of Empire: Militarism, Secrecy, and the End of the Republic*. New York: Henry Holt and Company, LLC:, p. 49.[63]
64. Baker, K. (2001, April). Another day of infamy. *American Heritage, 52*, 25.[64]
65. Thompson, M. (2000). *Raising Cain: Protecting the Emotional Life of Boys*. New York: The Ballantine Publishing Group, p. 99.[65]
66. Krakauer, J. (2003). *Under the Banner of Heaven: A Story of Violent Faith*. USA: DoubleDay, p. 27.[66]
67. Whitman, C. (2002, August 26). A strong climate plan. *Time, 160*, A48.[67]
68. Granatstein, L. (2003, May 19). Spring cleaning: Real simple eyes fashion fixes. *Mediaweek, 13*, 48.[68]
69. Huber, P. (1998, May 18). The energy diet that flopped. *Forbes, 161*, 306.[69]
70. Dumas, A. (1996). *The Count of Monte Cristo*. New York: Random House, Inc., p.365.[70]
71. Manley, W. (1994, April 1). You read it here first. *Booklist, 90*, 1408.[71]
72. Yoshino, K. (2003, March 12). Orange County: Letter proves its innocence, Anaheim utility says. *Los Angeles Times*, p. 3.[72]
73. Nesselson, L. (2003, April 21). Echelon: The secret power. *Variety, 390*, 27.[73]
74. Brown, D. (1998). *Digital Fortress*. New York: St. Martin's Press, p. 106.[74]
75. Johnson, D. (2002, August 16). Boston radio: Hub stations struggle with ads, 9/11 programming. *The Boston Herald*, p. 31.[75]
76. Phillips, D. (1996, July). Coming of age. *Entrepreneur, 24*, 98.[76]
77. Faber, M. (2002). *The Crimson Petal and the White*. Orlando, FL: Harcourt, Inc., p. 91.[77]
78. Davies, G. (2001, October 13). Celtic mixture provides intoxicating brew of emotions. *The Times* (London), Sport.[78]
79. Martin, L. (1991, April). Mr. Bowman's solution. *Saturday Evening Post, 263*, 46-53.[79]
80. Ingraham, Laura. (2007). *Power to the People*. Washington, DC: Regnery Publishing, p. 92.[80]
81. Daily News Yale (2003). *The Insider's Guide to the Colleges 20(30th Ed.)*. New York: The Yale Daily News Publishing Company, Inc./St. Martin's Press, p. 208.[81]

82. McChesney, R. W. & Nichols, J. (2003, February 24). Media democracy's moment: Suddenly, there are widespread discussions about the dangers of monopoly power. *The Nation, 276*, 16.[82]
83. Lepage, M. (2003, May 30). Minis are the stars in high-class caper. Donald Sutherland does his thing as veteran safecracker, then rats out his gang. Look out. *The Gazette*, p. D1.[83]
84. Marshall Goldsmith, Marshall and Reiter, Mark (2007). *What Got You Here Won't Get You There: How Successful People Become Even More Successful*. New York: Hyperion, p. 47.[84]
85. Levine, M. (2002). *A Mind at a Time*. New York: Simon and Schuster, p.174.[85]
86. Deam, J. (2003, February 10). The future of space? *The Denver Post*, p. 1.[86]
87. Stuertz, M. (2002, December 5). Green giant. Nobel laureate Norman Borlaug is credited with saving the lives of 1 billion people. So why is a small cadre of activist bent on tarnishing his legacy? *Dallas Observer*. Retrieved Dec. 17, 2003, from http://www.dallasobserver.com/issues/2002-12-05/feature.html/1/index.html[87]
88. Eliot, L. (1999) *What' Going on in There? How the Brain andMmind Develop in the First Five years of Life*. New York: Bantom Books, p.55.[88]
89. Velin, B. (2003, May 19). Gervin still loves game. *USA Today*, p. 7.[89]
90. Reid, T. R. (2003, May). The Sherpas. *National Geographic*, p. 71.[90]
91. Portman, J. (2003, January 21). The Fuehrer furore: Many people have attacked the movie Max, but Noah Taylor—who plays the young Hitler—tells Jamie Portman it's a valuable lesson in how evil takes root in a human being. *Ottawa Citizen*, p. B7.[91]
92. Gilman, S. J. (2001). Kiss *My Tiara: How to Rule the World As a Smartmouth Goddess*. New York: Warner Books, Inc., p.171.[92]
93. Schouten, H. (2003, April 10). Mill town. *The Dominion Post*, Features, General p. 5.[93]
94. Whiteside, K. (2002, August 20). Vol has "unfinished business." *USA Today*, p. 3C.[94]
95. Andrews, P. (1994, October). The press. *American Heritage, 45*, 36.[95]
96. Hamilton, J. (1986, December 15). A California doctor delivers good news to new moms with postpartum blues: It's curable. *People Weekly, 26*, 101.[96]
97. Brokaw, T. (1998). *The Greatest Generation*. New York: Random House, p.68.[97]
98. The road to Marathon. (2002, October 12). *The Economist*.[98]
99. O'Sullivan, J. (2002, November 25). A rendezvous with reality: Are immigrants needed to fill our jobs and make us grow? *National Review*, 54, p. A.[99]
100. Bleau, L. (2003, June 15). Detractors digging in against land proposal. *Tampa Tribune*, p. 4.[100]
101. Picknett, L. (1997). *The Templar Revelation: Secret Guardians of the True Identity of Christ*. New York: Touchstone, p. 97.[101]
102. Reibstein, L. (1997, August 25). The "cell from hell": Pfiesteria strikes again— in the Chesapeake Bay. *Newsweek, 130*, 63.[102]
103. Peters, J. (2003, April). Remission of gin: What 18th-century London can teach us about fighting vice. *Washington Monthly, 35*, 52.[103]
104. Miller, N. (2002, March 14). The film fest that turns a planet into a star. *The Washington Post*, p. 5.[104]
105. Sherwood, K. (1992). *Chakra Therapy: For Personal Growth and Healing*. St. Paul, MN: Llewellyn Publications, p. 89.[105]
106. Bryson, B. (2003). *A Short History of Nearly Everything*. New York: Random House, p. 219.[106]
107. The Hill: Senate GOP split over rules change on filibusters. (2003, May 14). *US Newswire*.[107]
108. Pryor, K. (1999). *Don't Shoot the Dog! The New Art of Teaching and Training*. New York: Bantam Books, p. 70.[108]
109. Acredolo, L. (2000). *Baby Minds: Brain-Building Games Your Baby Will Love*. New York: Bantam Books, p. xix.[109]
110. Martel, Y. (2001*)*. *Life of Pi*. Orlando, FL: Harcourt Books, Inc., p. 14.[110]

111. Nicholas, P. (2003, May 16). Hahn, chief rip council over funding. *Los Angeles Times*, p. 3.[111]
112. Ferguson, N. (N/A). *The Rise and Demise of the British World Order and the Lessons for Global Power.* Boulder, CO: Perseus Books Group, p. 301.[112]
113. Love, S. (1997, February 24). A surgeon's challenge: We need to better than the "slash, burn and poison" approach to breast cancer. *Newsweek, 129*, 60.[113]
114. Gutmann, D. (1998, Winter). The paternal imperative. *American Scholar, 67*, 118.[114]
115. MTV's World. (2002, February 18). *Business Week*, p. 40.[115]
116. Pedulla, T. (2003, May 13). Jockey lands on feet again. *USA Today*, p. 1.[116]
117. Briggs, C. (2003, May 16). Spiritual and sexual awakenings, a parent's decline, growing up with strangers—four women's critical life passages. *The Washington Post*, p. 13.[117]
118. Schneider, M. (2002, January 14). Disney re-learns its ABC's: New topper, asked changes may not be enough to right the ship. *Variety, 385*, 43.[118]
119. Berry, L. L. (1999). *Discovering the Soul of Service: The Nine Drivers of Sustainable Business Success.* New York: The Free Press, p. 40.[119]
120. Greene, Robert (2000). *The 48 Laws of Power.* New York: Viking Penguin, p. 328.[120]
121. Mortenson, Greg and Oliver Relin, David (2007). *Three Cups of Tea: One Man's Mission to Promote Peace . . . One School at a Time.* New York: The Penguin Group, p. 157.[121]
122. Baker, K. (2001, November-December). Our town: We've seen it (almost) all before. *American Heritage*, 52, 20.[122]
123. Gabaldon, D. (1991). *Outlander.* New York: Dell Publishing, p. 140.[123]
124. Lane, A. (2003, March 31). The prime minister. *The New Yorker, 79*, 034.[124]
125. Andrews, P. (2000, July 9). *The Seattle Times*, p.N3.[125]
126. Hart, J. (1990, September 17). Randall Jarrell: A literary life. *National Review, 42*, 48.[126]
127. Bart, P. (2003, January 6). The back lot. *Daily Variety, News*, p. 4.[127]
128. Cold War. (May 2000). *Harper's Magazine, 300*, 96.[128]
129. Jack Lynch (Ed.) (2004). *Samuel Johnson's Book of Insults: A Compendium of Snubs, Sneers, Slights and Effronteries from the 18th Century's Master.* New York: Walker and Co.[129]
130. Mallon, T. (2002, February). Books and Critics - Books: William Kennedy's greatest game - Roscoe has a lyricism and a gusto rarely achieved in serious American novels about politics. *The Atlantic Monthly, 289*, 93.[130]
131. Yerxa, D. (2002, May). The small chill: Rediscovering climate's impact on history. *Books and Culture, 8*, 40.[131]
132. Schulman, H. (2002, July 7). Giants rise up big time. *The San Francisco Chronicle*, p. B1.[132]
133. O'Reilly, S. (2001, September 1). Ulrike Kubatta: Profile. *Art Review*, p. 53.[133]
134. Dumb and dumber: Does it really matter if IQ scores go up or down? (2002, March 2). *New Scientist*, 173, 3.[134]
135. Newman, C. (1997, June). Cats: Nature's masterwork. *National Geographic, 191*, 54.[135]
136. Henry, G. (2001, February). Knowledge, learning, and experience. *American Artist, 65*, 24.[136]
137. Stephen E. D. & Heiman, S. (1998). *New Strategic Selling.* New York: Time Warner Books, p. 423.[137]
138. Daidoji, Y. (1999). *Code of the Samurai: A Modern Translation of the Bushido Shoshinsu.* Boston: Tuttle Publishing., p. 1.[138]
139. Ban Breathnach, S. (1995). *Simple Abundance: A Daybook of Comfort and Joy.* New York: Warner Books, Inc., p. 102.[139]
140. Robertson, D. (2003, May 26). Given time to ponder, Ausmus sees positives. *The Houston Chronicle*, Sports, p. 9.[140]

141. Perkins, S. (2003, April 5). Cannibal dinosaur known by its bones. *Science News, 163*, 211.[141]
142. Foucault, M. (1995). *Discipline and Punish: The Birth of the Prison*. New York: Random House, p. 40 (Book is quoting another source).[142]
143. Verducci, T. (2001, December 17). The power of two: Spurring each other on Curt Schilling and Randy Johnson carried Arizona to victory in the World Series—and enthralled a nation. *Sports Illustrated, 95*, 112.[143]
144. Klawans, S. (1995, June 26). Cannes '95. *The Nation, 260*, 936.[144]
145. Hildebrand, J. (2003, May 1). Schooled in patience. *Newsday*, p. A03.[145]
146. Celia, F. (2002, November-December). De-stress to decrease risk of diabetes: Exercise and diet aren't enough. *Psychology Today, 35*, 30.[146]
147. Thompson, M. (2000). *Raising Cain: Protecting the Emotional Life of Boys*. New York: The Ballantine Publishing Group, p. 244.[147]
148. Ambrose, S. (1996) *Undaunted Courage: Meriwether Lewis Thomas Jefferson and the Opening of the American West*. New York: Ambrose-Tubbs, Inc, p. 339.[148]
149. Frum, D. (June 16, 2003). What's right. *National Review, 55*, 56.[149]
150. Carnegie, D. (1984). *How to Stop Worrying and Start Living*. New York: Pocket Books, p. 100.[150]
151. Shapiro, L. M. (2002, August 15) Expunge him. Letters from the issue of Thursday, August 15, 2002. *Dallas Observer*. Retrieved December 17, 2003 from http://www.dallasobserver.com/issues/2002-08-15/letters.html/1/index.html.[151]
152. Bolch, B. (2003, February 16). Shrine Games: Pete Rose's career is a featured attraction in Cooperstown, even though he remains ineligible for the Hall of Fame. *Los Angeles Times*, p. 1.[152]
153. Krakauer, Jon (1999). *Into Thin Air: A Personal Account of the Mt. Everest Disaster*. New York: Anchor Books, p. 233.[153]
154. Beattie, Melody (1992). *Codependent No More: How to Stop Controlling Others and Start Caring for Yourself*. USA: Hazelden Foundation, p. 64.[154]
155. Dolgun, A. (1975) *Alexander Dolgun's Story*. New York: Alfred A. Knopf, Inc., p. 200.[155]
156. Darrach, B. (1987, December 14). Grand old Lillian Gish makes a big splash in The Whales of August. *People Weekly, 28*, 70-5.[156]
157. Collier, M. (2002). *Starting an eBay Business for Dummies*. New York: Wiley Publishing, Inc., p. 215.[157]
158. Wood, J. (2003, April). Cult of the master: The later Henry James was a master of technique. But how good a novelist was he? *The Atlantic Monthly, 291*, 102-9.[158]
159. Auletta, K. (2002, June 10). The Howell Doctrine. *The New Yorker*.[159]
160. Aetna: A long way to the recovery room. (2001, July 16). *Business Week*, p. 56.[160]
161. Weissbluth, M. (1999). *Healthy Sleep Habits, Happy Child*. New York: The Ballantine Publishing Group, p. 68.[161]
162. Faber, M. (2002). *The Crimson Petal and the White*. Orlando, FL: Harcourt, Inc, p. 563.[162]
163. Butcher, Jim (2001). *Grave Peril*. New American Library: New York, NY, p. 81.[163]
164. Cussler, Clive (2007). *The Chase by Clive*. Penguin Group: New York, NY, p. 198.[164]
165. Weber, D. (2003, February 20). Lopez lawyer files briefs blasting call for ouster as judge. *The Boston Herald*, p. O18.[165]
166. Ewers, J. (2002, September 16). Liza with a 3-year-old. *U. S. News and World Report*, p. 8.[166]
167. Ritter, J. (2003, February 10). Celebrating home-grown chocolate. *Chicago-Sun Times*, News Special Addition, p. 5.[167]
168. Platoni, K. (2003, June). Great expectations. *Smithsonian*, p. 61.[168]
169. Dawson, V. (2003, May). Comfort zone: A cardiganed Fred Rogers made every kid feel cozy and warm. *Smithsonian, 34*, 31.[169]

170. Anderson, L. (2003, May 16). Planning chief working to copy blueprint of previous job; Rutter modeling office after Howard operation; Anne Arundel. *The Baltimore Sun*, p. 1B.[170]
171. Caro, Robert (1975). *The Power Broker: Robert Moses and the Fall of New York*. New York: Random House, p. 278.[171]
172. Garrahan, M. (2002, October 1). My travel founder keeps the faith: Outgoing chairman believes business is in "good shape," says Matthew Garrahan. *Financial Times*, p. 24.[172]
173. McKee, R. (1997). *Story: Substance, Structure, Style and the Principles of Screenwriting*. New York: Harper Publishers, p. 43.[173]
174. Nemeth, M. (2002, July 15). Disappearing Saskatchewan: As farmers abandon their land, they're taking small-town life with them. *Maclean's*, p. 18.[174]
175. Anderson, R. (2002, September). Decipher the past. *New Scientist. 175*, 52-4.[175]
176. Groff, Lauren (20008). *The Monsters of Templeton*. New York: Hyperion, p. 65.[176]
177. Hamilton, A. (2002, September 16). Look who's on the telephone! The latest videophone looks great and is easy to set up. Will it succeed where all the rest have failed? *Time, 160*, 86.[177]
178. Reform's last gasp: European takeovers. (2003, May 24). *The Economist, 367*, 65.[178]
179. Ricks, T. (1996, November). Hazardous duty: America's most decorated living soldier reports from the front and tells it the way it is. *Washington Monthly, 28*, 55.[179]
180. Feurer, A. (2001, May 13). Reporter's Notebook; Violent Acts Recalled, by a Man of Few Words. *New York Times*, sec. 1, p. 32.[180]
181. Goltz, T. (2003). *Chechnya Diary: A War Correspondent's Story of Surviving the War in Chechnya*. New York: Thomas Dunne Books, p. 166.[181]
182. Evans, E. (2002, October 18). "General" portrait incomplete. *The Houston Chronicle*, p. 01.[182]
183. Alexander, C. (1977). *A Pattern Language: Towns, Buildings, Construction*. United States: Christopher Alexander, p. 356.[183]
184. Andrews. A. (2002). *The Traveler's Gift: Seven Decisions that Determine Personal Success*. Nashville, TN: Thomas Nelson, Inc., p. 136.[184]
185. Bennett, B. (2002, February 11). Get away to Taipei: Weekend wanderings. *Time International, 159*, 6.[185]
186. Weiner, Eric (2008). *The Geography of Bliss: One Grump's Search for the Happiest Places in the World*. Hachette Book Group: New York, NY, p. 12.[186]
187. Krakauer, J. (1997). *Eiger Dreams: Ventures among Men and Mountains*. New York: Anchor Books, p. 93.[187]
188. Perry, P. (1995, November-December). Teaching dogs new tricks. *Saturday Evening Post, 267*, 44-6.[188]
189. Fox, C. (2003, May 4). Architecture notes: A new name for GSU art school; Designation honors graduate. *The Atlanta Journal and Constitution*, p. 6M.[189]
190. Green, A. (2002, May 27). The magic basement. *The New Yorker, 78*, NA.[190]
191. Strauss, G. (2003, January 13). Birkenstock sticks toe in future with an eye to past. *USA Today*, p. 1B.[191]
192. Burton, Katherine (2007). *Hedge Hunters: Hedge Fund Masters on the Rewards, the Risk, and the Reckoning*. New York: Bloomberg Press, Front Cover.[192]
193. Browne, J. C. (1999). *The Sweet Potato Queens' Book of Love*. New York: Three Rivers Press, Back Matter.[193]
194. Pagels, E. (1989). *The Gnostic Gospels*. New York: Vintage Books, p. 152.[194]
195. McCall, K. (2003, June). In their corner: Focus your coaching efforts where they'll pack the most punch—on your top performers. *Entrepreneur, 31*, 79-81.[195]
196. Lowry. R. (2003, May 21). No reason to extend meaningless ban on assault weapons. *The Atlanta Journal-Constitution*, p. 19A.[196]
197. Bryson, B. (2003). *A Short History of Nearly Everything*. New York: Random House, Inc., p. 347.[197]

198. Tolle, Eckhart (2008). *A New Earth: Awakening to Your Life's Purpose*. New York: Penguin Group, p. 19.[198]
199. Wilson-Smith, A. (2003, April 21). The Media, unbound: There's a theory that true objectivity is impossible. So should we even try? *Maclean's*, p.4.[199]
200. Wellman, L. (2003, January 22). In the councils of war, nothing's cast in concrete. *The San Francisco Chronicle*, p. D10.[200]
201. Buckingham, M. (2001). *Now, Discover Your Strengths*. New York: The Free Press, p. 19.[201]
202. Glickman, R. (2002). *Optimal Thinking: How to Be Your Best Self*. New York: John Wiley and Sons, Inc., p. 178.[202]
203. Grossberger, L. (2002, October 7). Hold on to your parts. *Mediaweek, 12*, 34.[203]
204. Puig, C. (2003, March 21). Lunacy runs amok in "Dreamcatcher." *USA Today*, p. 10E.[204]
205. Ver Berkmoes, R. (1991, May-June). Tracking a killer: Why did seemingly healthy Amish babies suddenly sicken, become paralyzed, or die? Dr. Holmes Morton solved this mystery for the anguished parents. *Saturday Evening Post, 263*, 58. [205]
206. Reid, T. R. (2003, May). The Sherpas. *National Geographic*, p. 60.[206]
207. Hamm, S. (1994, April 4). The odd man out. *PC Week, 11*, A1-3.[207]
208. Ratto, R. (2003, May 25). Cure for road-weary club may be in the dirt. *The San Francisco Chronicle*, p. B1.[208]
209. Toole, J. K. (1980). A Confederacy of Dunces. Broadway, NY: *Grove Press*, p. 362.[209]
210. Spock, B. (1992). *Dr. Spock's Baby and Childcare (7th Ed.)*. New York: Simon and Schuster, Inc., p. 43.[210]
211. Risk of injury comes into play. Young athletes should not ignore preventive measures and exams. (2003, October 28). *Rockymountainnews.com*. Retrieved December 23, 2003, from the Rocky mountain News database (www.rockymountainnews.com).[211]
212. Keen, J. (2003, May 29). President's journey full of diplomatic challenges Europe, Mideast relations on line. *USA Today*, p. 6A.[212]
213. Vesilind, P. (1997, January). Sri Lanka. *National Geographic, 191*, p. 110.[213]
214. Nylund, E. (2003). First Strike (Halo). New York: The Random House Publishing Group, p. 122.[214]
215. Berger, E. (2003, May 4). Experts discuss nanotechnology for energy crisis. *The Houston Chronicle*, p.14A.[215]
216. Slywotzky, A. (2001, February 5). Standing tall in the tech slump: The dot-coms are collapsing around you. Don't gloat. Now's the time to remake your company. *Fortune, 143*, 176.[216]
217. Bryson, B. (2003). *A Short History of Nearly Everything*. New York: Broadway Books, p. 82.[217]
218. Vinay Menon Television, Associated Press. (2003, May 29). Everest in need of rest after 50 years of hikers. *Toronto Star*, p. A26.[218]
219. Witcover, J. (2003, May 14). McGovern: I am not an isolationist. *The Baltimore Sun*, p.13A.[219]
220. Corfield, P. (1997, December). Laughing at the learned. *History Today, 47*, 3-6.[220]
221. Nordlinger, J. (2003, January 27). Hootie vs. Hootie: The morality play surrounding Augusta National. *National Review*, 55. [221]
222. Collins, A. (2003). *The Draconomicon (Dungeons and Dragons)*. Renton, WA: Wizards of the Coast, Inc., p. 267.[222]
223. Newfield, J. (2002, October 7). The right's judicial juggernaut. *The Nation, 275*, 11.[223]
224. The X-Factor: With its eagerly awaited Xbox, Microsoft gets into the videogame-console business. (2001, November 5). *Newsweek*, p. 40B.[224]
225. Service, R. (2003, April 6). Life and soul of the party. *Sunday Times*, Features, Culture, p. 39.[225]
226. Woods, A. (2003, April 12). Elegia: Works by JS Bach, JC Bach, Biber, Blow, Purcell etc. White: Les Voix Baroques. *Music Week*, p. 24.[226]

227. Winter, J. (1998, November). A taste of ashes. *History Today*, p. 8.[227]
228. Sragow, M. (2003, May 14). Another whirl: Still stylish, but talky, "Matrix Reloaded" mostly runs in circles, killing time until the next sequel. *The Baltimore Sun*, p.1E..[228]b
229. Larson, E. (2003). *The Devil in the White City: Murder, Magic, and Madness at the Fair That Changed America*. New York: Crown Publishers, p. 287.[229]
230. Formichelli, L. (2002, January-February). Big disasters result in tiny babies. *Psychology Today*, 35, 21.[230]
231. Hope, C. (2003, May 3). Cruickshank has developed knack of reaching the annual meetings that others cannot reach. *The Herald*, p. 23.[231]
232. Kelleher, T. (1997, May 5). Jack Paar: As I was saying.... *People Weekly*, 47, 17.[232]
233. Chang, Jun (2003). *Wild Swans: Three Daughters of China*. New York: Touchstone, p. 496.[233]
234. Murphy, A. (1991, December 21). The grate one. *Sports Illustrated*, 75, 42-7.[234]
235. Cameron, W. B. (2003, February 8). A little "battle kill" nothing to fear. *Rocky Mountain News*, p. E2.[235]
236. Rauch, J. (2003, March). Caring for your introvert: The habits and needs of a little-understood group. (Personal File). *The Atlantic Monthly*, 291, 133-5.[236]
237. Cockburn, A. (2000, April). Yemen United. *National Geographic*, 197, 30.[237]
238. McGee, Harold (2004). *On Food and Cooking: The Science and Lore of the Kitchen*. New York: Scribner, p. 338.[238]
239. Bird, M. (2002, December 2). Death coast: After an aging tanker sinks off Spain, a vast slick of fuel oil destroys beaches, wildlife and fishermen's dreams. Could this disaster have been prevented? *Time International, 160*, 60.[239]
240. Dolgun, A. (1975) *Alexander Dolgun's Story*. New York: Alfred A. Knopf, Inc., p. 185.[240]
241. Shmith, M. (2003, June 1). Thanks for the mnemonics. *Sunday Age*, p. 16.[241]
242. Ignelzi, R. J. (2002, July 4). Techniques can help sharpen the mind. *The San Diego Union-Tribune*, p. E-1.[242]
243. Fitzgerald, R. (1974). *The Iliad*. USA: Anchor Books, p. 207.[243]
244. Paine, Thomas and Hook, Sidney (2003). *Common Sense, The Rights of Man and Other Essential Writings of Thomas Paine*. New York: Signet Classic, p. 364.[244]
245. Speelman, J. (2002, October 6). Escape, Games, Chess. *The Observer*, p. 19.[245]
246. Pollan, M. (2001). *The Botany of Desire: A Plant's-Eye View of the World*. New York: Random House, p. 85.[246]
247. Campos, C. (2003, March 17). Records' secrecy sought; Legislators fear criminals might use the documents. *The Atlanta Journal and Constitution*, p. 3B.[247]
248. Hill, J. (2003, May 29). Electronic games. *The Age, Green Guide*, Livewire, p. 16.[248]
249. James, B. (2003, May 21). County is struggling to find coaches. *St. Petersburg Times*, p. 6.[249]
250. Bonilla, D. & Martin, H. (2003, May 23). Los Angeles: Little drop-off seen in Memorial Day travel. *Los Angeles Times*, p. 3.[250]
251. Kulman, L., Firor, N. & Boser U. (2001, February 26). Job jitters? Stay calm. Hiring still outstrips firing. *U. S. News and World Report, 130*, 56.[251]
252. *The World Almanac and Book of Facts 2004*. (2004). New York: World Almanac Books, p. 179.[252]
253. Wallach, J. (1999). *Desert Queen: The Extraordinary Life of Gertrude Bell: Adventurer, Adviser to Kings, Ally of Lawrence of Arabia*. New York: Anchor Books, p. 299.[253]
254. Daidoji, Y. (1999). *Code of the Samurai: A Modern Translation of the Bushido Shoshinsu*. Boston: Tuttle Publishing, p.6.[254]
255. Loewen, J. W. (1995). *Lies My Teacher Told Me: Everything Your American History Textbook Got Wrong*. New York: Touchstone, p. 283.[255]
256. Ross, Alex (2007). *The Rest Is Noise: Listening to the Twentieth Century*. New York: Farrar, Straus and Giroux, p. 333. [256]

257. Spiros, D. (2003, May 12). Looking for a weakness; Riddling him with shots was not the answer. But Wild players insist that Anaheim goalie Jean-Sebastien Giguere can be solved. *Star Tribune*, p. 4S.[257]
258. Roessing, W. (1988, April). The madcap side of pro golf. *Saturday Evening Post, 260*, 48.[258]
259. Baldwin, T. & Bennett, R. (2002, November 16). Ministers seek more control of firefighters. *The Times, Home News*, 14.[259]
260. Finlay, V. (2002). *Color: A Natural History of the Palette*. New York: The Ballantine Publishing Group, p. 50.[260]
261. Bronson, P. (2002). *What Should I Do with My Life?* New York: Random House, p. 139.[261]
262. DiManno, R. (2003, April 21). Hunt for the disappeared leads to hellish tunnels. *Toronto Star*, p. A02.[262]
263. West, J. L. (2000, Spring). Annotating Mr. Fitzgerald. *American Scholar, 69*, 82.[263]
264. Rau, J. (2003, May 1). Can Pataki win back allies? Rift widens as governor, Senate follow different agendas. *Newsday*, p. A22.[264]
265. Friedman, T. L. (2000). *The Lexus and the Olive Tree: Understanding Globalization*. New York: Random House, Inc., p. 436.[265]
266. Langworthy, D. (1996, September). Inside the tent. *American Theatre, 13*, 17.[266]
267. Abbey, E. (1968). *Desert Solitaire*. New York: Ballantine Books, p. 150.[267]
268. Semler, G. (1995, September 25). A year in Iberia. *Forbes, 156*, S95-101.[268]
269. Kennedy, K. (1999, November 9). Inside the NHL. *Sports Illustrated, 91*, 160.[269]
270. Petroski, H. (1992). *To Engineer Is Human: The Role of Failure in Successful Design*. New York: Vintage Books, p. 177.[270]
271. Williams, P. (2003, April 14). Codes of etiquette. *The Nation, 276*, 10.[271]
272. Schultz, Patricia (2007). *1,000 Places to See in the U.S.A. & Canada Before You Die*. New York: Workman Publishing, p. 436.[272]
273. Carnegie, D. (1981). *How to Win Friends and Influence People*. New York: Simon and Schuster, Inc., p. 82.[273]
274. Nelson, S. (2003, May 17). State looks at deregulating auto rates ideas for change solicited from task force, others. *The Boston Globe*, p. C1.[274]
275. Sebold, A. (2002). *The Lovely Bones*. USA: Alice Sebold, p. 27.[275]
276. Ward, R. (2003, March-April). Moody teens: A diagnosis, but no cure. *Psychology Today, 36*, 24.[276]
277. Sellers, P. (2003, May 26). Ted Turner is a worried man. His media career is gone with the wind. His faith in the United Nations looks naive. He thinks humanity's on the verge of extinction, and he's down to his last billion. *Fortune, 147*, 124.[277]
278. Builder named to Order of Canada. (2003, April 26). *Toronto Star*, p. J06.[278]
279. Park, E. (1991, January). Around the mall and beyond. *Smithsonian, 21*, 22-5.[279]
280. Peck, M. S. (1978). *The Road Less Traveled, 25th Anniversary Edition: A New Psychology of Love, Traditional Values and Spiritual Growth*. New York: Touchstone, p. 24.[280]
281. Lemonick, M. (2003, March 31). Feb. 28, 1953, Eureka: The double helix. *Time, 161*, A30.[281]
282. Levine, M. (2002). *A Mind at a Time*. New York: Simon and Schuster, p. 286.[282]
283. Hopper, A. (2002, December 12). Alice's adventures in wonderland: Christmas review: Keswick. *The Stage*, p. 22.[283]
284. Kotter, J. P. (1996) *Leading Change*. Cambridge, MA: Harvard Business School Press, p. 3.[284]
285. Loewen, J. W. (1995) Lies My Teacher Told Me. Everything Your American History Textbook Got Wrong. New York: Touchstone, p. 38, [285]
286. Bryson B. (2003). *A Short History of Nearly Everything*. Broadway Books, p. 217.[286]
287. Pence, A. (2003 February 19). Not all orchids are difficult to care for. *The San Francisco Chronicle*, p. 6WB.[287]
288. Klawans, S. (2002, September). The play's the thing. *The Nation, 275*, 44.[288]

289. Goleman, D. (1998). *Working with Emotional Intelligence.* New York:Bantam Books, p. 184.[289]
290. Springer, S. (2003, March 20). Celticsnotebook:They'remisfiringfromlongrange. *The Boston Globe*, p. F5. [290]
291. Foundas, S. (2003, May 5). I Witness. *Variety*, 390, 37.[291]
292. Adams, D. (2002). The Ultimate Hitchhiker's Guide to the Galaxy. USA: Ballantine Publishing Group, p. 8.[292]
293. Chu, D. (1986, June 9). Rice isn't just for weddings: Judy Moscovitz used it to diet from 275 lbs. to a svelte 123. *People Weekly*, p. 133.[293]
294. Senge, P. M. (1990). *The Fifth Discipline.* New York: Bantam Doubleday Dell Publishing Group, p. 295.[294]
295. Rosen, M. (1993, June 21). The Rivers run together: After a period of estrangement, Joan Rivers and daughter Melissa share life, laughs and love. *People Weekly, 39,* 70-6.[295]
296. Sheppard, R. (2003, March 24). Cracking the genetic code: It's 50 years since two brash, ambitious scientists unveiled the double helix. *Maclean's*, p. 48.[296]
297. Engardio, J. (2000, January 5). Charity begins @ home; A young software engineer has a plan to teach Silicon Valley to change its tightfisted ways. *SF Weekly*, Features.[297]
298. Brandt, A. (1997, February 24). One connected quartet. *Forbes, 159,* S65-76.[298]
299. Sokol, M. (2003, June 6). The fine art of opening a business in Keystone. *St. Petersburg Times*, p. 1.[299]
300. Senge, P. M. (1990). *The Fifth Discipline.* New York: Doubleday, p. 19.[300]
301. Collins, A., Willismes, S. & Wyatt J. (1993). *The Draconomicon (Dungeons and Dragons).* Renton, WA: Wizards of the Coast, Inc., p. 264.[301]
302. Cialdini, R. B. (1993). *Influence: The Psychology of Persuasion.* New York: Wlliam Morrow and Company, Inc., p. Back Matter.[302]
303. Covey, S. R. (1989). *Seven Habits of Highly Effective People.* New York: Fireside, p. 209.[303]
304. Koeppel, F. (2003, March 16). The wizard of artistic enigma - Barney concocts an exotic potion and labels it "the cremaster cycle." *The Commercial Appeal*, p. F1.[304]
305. Tozer, T. (1996, May-June). Letting Michael be Michael ... a 12-year-old with 4 Guinness records. *Saturday Evening Post*, p. 268.[305]
306. Platoni, K. (2003, June). Great expectations. *Smithsonian*, p. 61.[306]
307. Magazine poll ranks city 13th as an arts destination. (2003, June 3). *Pittsburgh Post-Gazette*, p. B-2.[307]
308. Pink, Daniel H. (2006). *A Whole New Mind: Why Right-Brainers Will Rule the Future.* New York: The Berkley Publishing Group, p. 57. [308]
309. McCullough, D. (2001). *The Great Bridge: The Epic Story of the Building of the Brooklyn Bridge.* New York: Simon & Schuster, chapter 1.[309]
310. McGee, Harold (2004). *On Food and Cooking: The Science and Lore of the Kitchen.* New York: Scribner, p. 338.[310]
311. Davis, W. (1999, August). Vanishing cultures. *National Geographic,* 196, p. 62.[311]
312. Leigh, R. (1983). *Holy Blood, Holy Grail.* New York: Dell Publishing, p. 36.[312]
313. Neville, K. (1988). *The Eight.* New York: The Ballantine Publishing Group, p. 158.[313]
314. Roberts, C. (2004). *Founding Mothers: The Women Who Raised Our Nation.* New York: HarperCollins Publishers Inc., p. 32.[314]
315. Zinn, H. (2003). *A People's History of the United States: 1492-Present.* New York: HarperCollins Publishers Inc., p. 158.[315]
316. Sunny Jim just can't say no. (2003, May 23). *The Dominion Post* (Wellington, New Zealand), p. 2.[316]
317. Homegrown help. (1998, July 6). *People Weekly,* 49, 12.[317]
318. Moffat, S. (1996, September 30). Hong Kong Jockey Club. *Fortune, 134,* 73.[318]
319. Weiss, B. (1988). *Many Lives, Many Masters.* New York: Simon and Schuster, Inc., p. 24.[319]

320. Van Gelder, L. (2002, April 2). Footlights. *New York Times*, p. E1.[320]
321. Woodson, J. (2003, May 20). Triple-Murderer gets death; Alfred Flores, who killed teens for refusing to join his gang, laughs at the survivors. *Los Angeles Times*, p. 1.[321]
322. Martel, Y. (2001). *Life of Pi*. Orlando, FL: Harcourt, Inc., p. 285.[322]
323. Wood, C. (2000, February). The Web is a hacker's playground. *PC World, 18*, 33.[323]
324. Brown, S. (1991). *Breath of Scandal*. New York: Warner Books, Inc., p. 148.[324]
325. Ellis, J. J. (2000). *Founding Brothers: The Revolutionary Generation*. New York: Alfred A. Knopf, p. 201.[325]
326. Dirda, M. (2002, July-August). Great Granny Webster. *The Atlantic Monthly, 290*, 189.[326]
327. Martel, Y. (2001). *Life of Pi*. Orlando, FL: Harcourt, Inc., p. 212.[327]
328. Rosenthal, A. (2003, February 10). Bloody, brutal and grimly moral: Amy Rosenthal enjoys a thrillingly contemporary revenge tragedy. *New Statesman, 132*, 46.[328]
329. Prose, F. (1997, April 14). After the madness: A judge's own prison memoir. *People Weekly, 47*, 35.[329]
330. Bornstein, D. (2004). *How to Change the World: Social Entrepreneurs and the Power of New Ideas*. New York: Oxford University Press, Inc., p. 44.[330]
331. Cochrane, J. & Kola, K. (2002, December 9). The parent killer. *Newsweek International*, p. 25.[331]
332. Lansing, A. (1959). *Endurance: Shackleton's Incredible Voyage*. New York: Carroll and Graf Publishers, p. 4.[332]
333. Buckingham, M. (1999). *First, Break All the Rules: What the World's Greatest Managers Do Differently*. New York, NY: Simon and Schuster, Appendix E.[333]
334. Corcoran, E. (2000, October 2). Go forth and publish. *Forbes, 166*, 170.[334]
335. Phillips, B. (1999). *Body for Life: 12 Weeks to Mental and Physical Strength*. New York: HarperCollins, p. 74.[335]
336. Anderson, W. (1989, July-August). In the footsteps of the Lincolns. *Saturday Evening Post, 261*, 64.[336]
337. Dolgun, A. (1975) *Alexander Dolgun's Story*. New York: Alfred A. Knopf, Inc., p. 25.[337]
338. Derek, C. B. (2001). The effect of admissions test preparation: Evidence from NELS: 88. *Chance, 14*, 10.[338]
339. Stipp, D. (2003, May 26). Biotech's Billion Dollar Breakthrough: A technology called RNAi has opened the door to major new drugs. Already it's revolutionizing gene research. *Fortune, 147*, 96.[339]
340. Schwartz, J. (2003, June 1). San Marcos plans to honor jazz great, native son Durham. *The Houston Chronicle*, p. 38-A.[340]
341. Maguire, Gregory (2000). *Confessions of an Ugly Stepsister*. New York:Harpr Collins, p. 182.[341]
342. Saramago, J. (1995). *Blindness*. Orlando, FL: Harcourt, Inc, p. 101-102.[342]
343. Schindehette, S. & Dodd, J. (2002, June 24). The baby tamer: Dr. Harvey Karp claims he can calm almost any crying newborn—and you can too. *People Weekly, 57*, 149.[343]
344. Aubin, B. (2002, July 22). At the crossroads: How long can the country keep up its balancing act? *Maclean's*, p. 28.[344]
345. Liss, D. (2000). *A Conspiracy of Paper*. New York: The Ballantine Publishing Group, p. 150.[345]
346. Carnegie, D. (1956). *How to Develop Self-Confidence and Influence People*. New York: Simon and Schuster Inc., p. 55.[346]
347. Jacobson, A. (2003, May 20). Out of the shadow. *Newsday*, p. B06.[347]
348. Simon, J. (1996, September 30). A little lower than festive. *National Review, 48*, 67.[348]
349. Eire, C. (2003). *Waiting for Snow in Havana: Confessions of a Cuban Boy*. New York: The Free Press, p. 102.[349]

350. Peck, M. S. (2003). *The Road Less Traveled, 25th Anniversary Edition: A New Psychology of Love, Traditional Values and Spiritual Growth*. New York: Simon and Schuster, Inc., p. 137.[350]
351. Bryson, B. (1999). *I'm a Stranger Here Myself: Notes on Returning to America after 20 Years Away*. New York: Broadway Books, p. 215.[351]
352. Johnson, W. & Lilley, J. (1992, August 10). Swimmers for sale. *Sports Illustrated, 77*, 46.[352]
353. Fields-Meyer, T. (1999, December 20). Dead end: A moment of anger in rush-hour traffic costs the life of a mother of three. *People Weekly, 52*, 131.[353]
354. Moss, E. L. (2000, January). How drawing and driving are alike. *American Artist, 64*, 42.[354]
355. Kurcinka, M. S. (1991). *Raising Your Spirited Child: A Guide for Parents Whose Child Is More Intense, Sensitive, Perceptive, Persistent, Energetic*. New York: HarperCollins Publishers, Inc., p. 129.[355]
356. Maister, D. (2000). *The Trusted Advisor*. New York: Simon and Schuster, p. 117.[356]
357. Loehr, J. (2003). *The Power of Full Engagement: Managing Energy, Not Time, is the Key to High Performance and Personal Renewal*. New York: Free Press, p. 82.[357]
358. Krakauer, J. (2003). *Under the Banner of Heaven: A Story of Violent Faith*. New York: Doubleday, p. 325.[358]
359. Lencioni, P. M. (2002). *The Five Dysfunctions of a Team: A Leadership Fable*. New York: Jossey-Bass, p. 64.[359]
360. Shatz, A. (2002, March 24). Music: A jazz diva who's losing interest in jazz. *New York Times*, p. 1.[360]
361. Kreiter, T. (1997, May-June). Salt savvy. *Saturday Evening Post, 269*, 26.[361]
362. Lawlet, A. (2003, June). Iraq's treasures. *Smithsonian*, p. 49.[362]
363. Bennett, B. (2001, July 16). Annals of conservatism: We are all God's creatures—yes, even the pigeons. *Time International, 158*, 10.[363]
364. Hilton, M. (2000, May). Smoking gun. *History Today, 50*, 36.[364]
365. Rodman, S. (2003, April 4). Music: The kids are alright. Rockers' offspring take center stage. *The Boston Herald*, p. S03.[365]
366. McCullough, D. (1992). *Truman*. New York: Simon and Schuster, p. 357.[366]
367. Siegfried, D. (2002, November 1). Witt, James Lee and Morgan, James. Stronger in the broken places: Nine lessons for turning crisis into triumph. *Booklist, 99*, 463.[367]
368. Stuller, J. (1984, October). Lee Iacocca and an America that's back on its feet. *Saturday Evening Post, 256*, 46-51.[368]
369. Lawlet, A. (2003, June). Iraq's treasures. *Smithsonian*, p. 53.[369]
370. Hoffer, R. (1999, January 18). Haunted. *Sports Illustrated, 90*, 62.[370]
371. Padilla, D. (2003, May 14). Feisty Manuel sticks up for Thomas. *Chicago Sun-Times*, p. 145.[371]
372. Barlow, J. P. (2002, October 7). Why spy? *Forbes, ASAP, 170*, 42.[372]
373. Devil Rays to test Piniella's patience: Leading off players to watch spotlight battle: Chicago connection the lineup numbers game. (2003, March 14). *Chicago Sun-Times*, p. 140.[373]
374. Bergman, B. (1998, October 12). Show-no-mercy-Mercer: In his new show, Rick Mercer once again plays it nasty. *Maclean's, 111*, 73.[374]
375. Communities. (2003, April 17). *Plain Dealer*, p. B3.[375]
376. McClure, S. (2002, August 24). Hyde out. (Global Music Pulse). *Billboard, 114*, 57.[376]
377. Sherman, M. (2003, March 7). Visa takes measures to curb identity theft: Credit-card companies to require new machines to display only four digits. *The Gazette*, p. B2.[377]
378. Schneier, B. (2000). *Secrets and Lies: Digital Security in a Networked World*. New York: John Wiley and Sons, Inc., p.209.[378]
379. Neal, V. (2000, April). The fall guys. *Entrepreneur, 28*, 26.[379]
380. Wiegand, D. (2003, May 23). HBO constructs a magnificent, richly detailed "House": Maggie Smith steals show in subtle role. *The San Francisco Chronicle*, p. D2.[380]

381. Covey, S. R. (1994). *First Things First: To Live, to Love, to Learn, to Leave a Legacy.* New York: Simon and Schuster, Inc., p. 104.[381]
382. Murphy, J. (2000). *The Power of Your Subconscious Mind* (Rev. Ed.). New York: Bantam Books, p.177.[382]
383. Gottman, J. M. (1999). *The Seven Principles for Making Marriage Work: A Practical Guide from the Country's Foremost Relationship Expert.* New York: Three Rivers Press, p. 9.[383]
384. A critical eye. (2001, March). *American Artist, 65,* 8.[384]
385. Eggers, D. (2001). *A Heartbreaking Work of Staggering Genius.* New York: Random House, p. 316.[385]
386. Blevins, J. (2003, May 27). Sweet venture tastes great, less ingredients Denverite's nutrition bars a natural passion for unprocessed, healthy and, yes, tasty food inspired successful creation. *The Denver Post,* p. C-01.[386]
387. Ross, D. (1992, September-October). The patient who couldn't speak. *Saturday Evening Post, 264,* 64.[387]
388. Underhill, P. (1999). *Why We Buy: The Science Of Shopping.* New York: Simon and Schuster, p. 68.[388]
389. Gillen, M. (2000, September 9). UMG, MP3 court case hinges on "willfulness." *Billboard,* p. 112.[389]
390. Fernandez-Armesto, F. (1996, March). Times and tides. *History Today, 46,* 4.[3]
391. Global briefing. (2001, October 9). *Time, 158,* B7.[391]
392. Leshko, A. (2002, August). Just a snapshot? *Smithsonian,* p. 19.[392]
393. Botkin, S. C. (2003). *Lower Your Taxes - Big Time! Wealth-Building, Tax Reduction Secrets from an IRS Insider.* New York: McGraw Hill, p. 105.[393]
394. Slavin, P. (1996, May). The information age and the civil society: An interview with Jeremy Rifkin. *Phi Delta Kappan, 77,* 607.[394]
395. Rushin, S. (1997, March 3). Inside the moat. *Sports Illustrated, 86,* 68.[395]
396. Saving the forest for the trees. (2000, November 20). *Business Week,* p. 62.[396]
397. Lane, A. (2002, August 12). Field trip. *New Yorker.*[397]
398. Leach, M. (2003, June 15). Tough Romans Apparently Liked Flowers. *Columbus Dispatch,* p. 01I.[398]
399. Shaughnessy, D. (2003, May 21). It seems that Lyon has closed in on the job. *The Boston Globe,* p. F5.[399]
400. Kreisman, J. J. (1989). *I Hate You, Don't Leave Me: Understanding the Borderline Personality.* Los Angeles: Price Stern Sloan, Inc., p. 106.[400]

Bibliography

Atkinson, R. C. (1975). Mnemotechnics in second-language learning. *American Psychologist, 30*, 821-828.

Avila, E. & Sadoski, M. (1996). Exploring new applications of the keyword method to acquire English vocabulary. *Language Learning, 46*, 379-395.

Carney, R. N. & Levin, J. R. (1998). Coming to term with the keyword method in Introductory Psychology: A "neuromnemonic" example. *Teaching of Psychology, 25,* 132-134.

Harper Collins Webster's Dictionary. (2003). New York: Harper Collins Publishers.

Jones, M. J., Levin, M. E., Levin, J.R. & Beitzel, B.D. (2000). Can vocabulary-learning strategies and pair-learning formats be profitably combined? *Journal of Educational Psychology, 92*, 256-262.

Levin, J. R. (1982). Pictures as prose learning devices. In A. Flammer & W. Kintsch (ed.). *Discourse Processing-Advances in Psychology.* New York: North-Holland Publishing Company. p. 412-444.

Levin, J. R. (1986). Four cognitive principles of learning-strategy instruction. *Educational Psychologist, 21*, 3-17.

Levin, J. R. (1983). Pictorial strategies for school learning:Practical illustrations. In M. Pressley & J.R. Levin (Eds.), *Cognitive strategy research: Educational applications* (pp. 213-237). New York: Springer-Verlag.

Levin, J.R. (1981). The Mnemonic'80s: Keywords in the classroom. *Educational Psychologist, 16*, 65-82.

Lysynchuk, L. & Pressley, M. (1990). Vocabulary (ch.4) in *Cognitive strategy instruction that really improves children's academic performance.* Cabridge, MA: Brookline Books.

Mastropieri, M. A. & Scruggs, T. E. (1991). *Teaching students ways to remember.* BrooklineBooks: Cambridge, MA.

Merriam Webster's online dictionary. Retrieved from www.merriamwebster.com.

Procter, P. (Ed.). (1995). *Cambridge International Dictionary of English.* Cambridge. United Kingdom: Cambridge University Press.

Sternberg, R. J. (1986) Beyond IQ: *A triarchic theory of Human inteligence.* Yale University Press: New Haven, CT.

The American Heritage Dictionary. (2001). Boston, NY: Houghton Mifflin Company.

Wang, A. Y. & Thomas, H. T. (1995). Effect of keywords on long-term retention: Help or hindrance? *Journal of Educational Psychology, 87*, 468-475.

Review Answers

Section 1

Crossword Puzzle
Across: 3- amiable 5- bereft 6- abeyance 10- abet 11- abstruse
12- assiduous 13- amalgamate 6- alacrity 17- aver
Down: 1- arbiter 2- belie 4- bane 5- bemuse 6- anomaly
7- apocryphal 8- baleful 9- bellicose 12- attenuation
14- abrogate 15- audacious

Multiple Choice
1-b. bereft 2-d. assiduous 3-d. abstruse 4-b. amalgamated
5-c. baleful 6-a. abrogated 7-a. belie 8-b. alacrity
9-a. averred 10-d. abetted 11-a. bellicose 12-a. abeyance
13-b. anomaly 14-c. apocryphal 15-b. amiable 16-d. audacious
17-a. bane 18-d. bemused 19-c. arbiter 20-a. attenuated

Matching
1-J 2-E 3-C 4-T 5-K 6-A 7-M 8-L 9-P 10-N 11-O 12-F
13-I 14-Q 15-H 16-S 17-D 18-B 19-R 20-G

Section 2

Crossword Puzzle
Across: 2- delineate 4- candor 6- conciliatory 7- conundrum
9- daunt 10- castigate 13- cacophony 14- craven 15- boor
16- capricious 17- bombastic
Down: 1- chagrin 3- capitulate 4- credulous 5- cognizant
8- deleterious 9- debacle 11- contumacious 12- countermand
15- broach

Multiple Choice
1-d. boor 2-a. bombastic 3-b. chagrin 4-b. daunted
5-b. cacophony 6-d. candor 7-a. capricious 8-b. contumacious
9-d. castigated 10-c. broach 11-b. capitulated 12-b. conciliatory
13-d. debacle 14-a. deleterious 15-c. conundrum
16-a. delineates 17-a. craven 18-c. credulous
19-c. countermanded 20-b. cognizant

Matching
1-M 2-T 3-O 4-G 5-S 6-F 7-K 8-I 9-R 10-J 11-B 12-L
13-Q 14-P 15-A 16-C 17-N 18-H 19-E 20-D

Section 3

Crossword Puzzle
Across: 2- demur 4- dogmatic 6- discursive 9- derision
10- efficacious 11- embroil 13- demagogue 15- dulcet
17- eclectic
Down: 1- denigration 2- didactic 3- disparage 5- encumber
7- empirical 8- discordant 9- diffidence 12- dilatory
14- effrontery 15- duplicity 16- effluvia

Multiple Choice
1-c. dulcet 2-c. denigration 3-a. efficacious 4-a. effrontery
5-d. duplicity 6-a. derision 7-c. empirical 8-a. didactic
9-b. diffidence 10-a. embroiled 11-b. dilatory 12-a. encumbered
13-c. eclectic 14-c. dogmatic 15-b. effluvia 16-a. discursive
17-d. discordant 18-b. demagogue 19-d. demurred
20-a. disparaged

Matching
1-C 2-O 3-T 4-B 5-S 6-L 7-J 8-R 9-G 10-D 11-H 12-Q
13-A 14-E 15-N 16-F 17-K 18-P 19-I 20-M

Section 4

Crossword Puzzle
Across: 1- enervate 4- erudite 7- exhortation 8- evanescent
11- extricate 13- esoteric 15- fallacious 16- feckless
18- fastidious
Down: 1- ephemeral 2- exculpate 3- extenuating 5- evince
6- exacerbate 9- exonerate 10- equivocal 12- fatuous
14- epitome 15- fabricate 17- enigma

Multiple Choice
1-d. epitome 2-c. exacerbated 3-a. fastidious 4-b. exonerated
5-b. enigma 6-a. fallacious 7-d. erudite 8-c. fatuous
9-c. extenuating 10-a. ephemeral 11-c. equivocal 12-b. esoteric
13-b. evinced 14-d. exculpated 15-b. evanescent
16-a. exhortation 17-c. extricate 18-a. feckless 19-c. enervated
20-d. fabricated

Matching Review
1-T 2-A 3-G 4-Q 5-M 6-B 7-S 8-K 9-I 10-D 11-N 12-H
13-C 14-L 15-O 16-F 17-E 18-P 19-R 20-J

Chapter 5

Crossword Puzzle
Across: 1- florid 3- garrulous 5- gregarious 6- frenetic 8- flout
9- imprecation 11- hedonistic 13- hapless 14- hone
16- impetuous
Down: 1- fulsome 2- furtive 4- impute 5- gratuitous 6- foment
7- inane 10- impervious 12- incongruous 14- heretic 15- guile

Multiple Choice
1-c. hedonists 2-c. florid 3-b. hapless 4-b. impervious
5-b. imputed 6-b. heretic 7-b. garrulous 8-a. flouted
9-c. gratuitous 10-a. fomented 11-a. furtive 12-a. frenetic
13-b. fulsome 14-c. gregarious 15-d. guile 16-c. hone
17-d. inane 18-d. incongruous 19-d. impetuous
20-a. imprecations

Matching
1-F 2-J 3-O 4-H 5-K 6-I 7-S 8-A 9-L 10-B 11-Q 12-N
13-E 14-P 15-M 16-C 17-G 18-D 19-R 20-T

Chapter 6

Crossword Puzzle
Across: 1- lachrymose 3- intractable 4- incursion
5- loquacious 8- maladroit 11- ingenuous 13- inimical
14- insolvent 15- lionize 16- inure
Down: 1- lugubrious 2- laconic 3- indolent 6- indefatigable
7- intransigence 9- indomitable 10- lassitude 11- irascible
12- intrepid 14- innocuous

Multiple Choice
1-a. insolvent 2-a. maladroit 3-d. indolent 4-c. laconic
5-d. lugubrious 6-b. inured 7-a. indomitable 8-b. inimical
9-d. intractable 10-c. innocuous 11-a. irascible 12-c. lachrymose
13-a. intransigence 14-b. lassitude 15-d. lionized
16-d. loquacious 17-c. indefatigable 18-c. incursions
19-c. ingenuous 20-a. intrepid

Matching
1-I 2-D 3-T 4-M 5-N 6-R 7-F 8-C 9-P 10-G 11-B 12-S
13-A 14-J 15-K 16-L 17-O 18-E 19-Q 20-G

Chapter 7

Crossword Puzzle
Across: 2- obstreperous 7- panegyric 8- pariah 10- mnemonic
11- munificence 15- opulent 17- mendicant 18- obsequious
Down: 1- obfuscate 3- palliate 4- multifarious 5- nefarious
6- paradigm 7- parsimony 9- ossify 10- malevolent
12- melancholy 13- nascent 14- officious 16- nadir

Multiple Choice
1-d. nefarious 2-c. nascent 3-c. multifarious 4-c. nadir
5-c. pariah 6-b. obstreperous 7-b. obfuscating 8-b. opulent
9-c. obsequious 10-b. mendicants 11-d. paradigms 12-a. ossify
13-c. palliate 14-d. panegyric 15-a. parsimony 16-b. officious
17-a. malevolent 18-a. mnemonic 19-b. melancholy
20-b. munificence

Matching
1-A 2-N 3-S 4-G 5-J 6-B 7-T 8-L 9-R 10-K 11-C 12-H
13-O 14-E 15-Q 16-P 17-I 18-M 19-D 20-F

Section 8

Crossword Puzzle
Across: 7- polemic 8- philanthropic 9- peregrination 10- pique
12- precocious 14- proclivity 15- pellucid 16- pernicious
Down: 1- predilection 2- precipitous 3- phlegmatic 4- profusion
5- petulant 6- placate 8- perfunctory 9- ponderous
10- pretentious 11- prodigious 12- paucity 13- perfidious

Multiple Choice
1-c. ponderous 2-b. placate 3-a. polemic 4-b. piqued
5-d. precocious 6-c. precipitous 7-d. profusion 8-d. predilection
9-c. proclivity 10-d. pernicious 11-c. peregrinate 12-b. paucity
13-d. prodigious 14-a. pretentious 15-d. petulant
16-a. philanthropic 17-c. perfunctory 18-a. pellucid
19-d. phlegmatic 20-d. perfidious

Matching
1-C 2-P 3-I 4-K 5-A 6-G 7-M 8-T 9-D 10-L 11-S 12-F
13-B 14-N 15-H 16-R 17-O 18-Q 19-J 20-E

Section 9

Crossword Puzzle
Across: 2- prolific 4- sanguine 9- quixotic 11- pundit 12- salutary 14- raucous 16- provocation 17- purport
Down: 1- seminal 3- sanctimonious 5- sagacity 6- salient 7- ribald 8- protract 10- reticent 13- raconteur 14- retrograde 15- reprobate 16- prosaic 18- ramify

Multiple Choice
1-c. protracted 2-d. provocation 3-b. sanctimonious
4-d. reprobate 5-a. reticent 6-a. retrograde 7-b. raconteur
8-c. salient 9-a. salutary 10-c. ribald 11-b. sanguine
12-d. seminal 13-a. pundit 14-c. ramified 15-d. sagacious
16-a. quixotic 17-b. prolific 18-b. purported 19-d. prosaic
20-d. raucous

Matching
1-G 2-F 3-N 4-E 5-D 6-C 7-L 8-M 9-P 10-Q 11-R 12-O
13-B 14-A 15-T 16-K 17-H 18-J 19-S 20-I

Section 10

Crossword Puzzle
Across: 4- turpitude 6- voluble 8- temerity 11- sophistry 14- truncate 17- soporific 18- serendipity 19- ungainly
Down: 1- tawdry 2- supersede 3- zealot 5- transient 7- sycophant 9- stymie 10- superfluous 12- surreptitious 13- sequester 14- tenacity 15- vapid 16- vacillate

Multiple Choice
1-a. sequestered 2-c. tawdry 3-b. supersede 4-a. ungainly
5-a. stymied 6-a. serendipity 7-a. temerity 8-c. vacillates
9-b. sophistry 10-a. vapid 11-b. surreptitious 12-c. sychophant
13-d. transient 14-a. truncates 15-b. turpitude 16-d. voluble
17-d. soporofic 18-c. tenacity 19-c. superfluous 20-d. zealot

Matching
1-P 2-I 3-L 4-R 5-E 6-D 7-T 8-G 9-K 10-M 11-F 12-B
13-A 14-J 15-S 16-O 17-N 18-Q 19-H 20-C

Index

Index

Introduction
auditory learner, xiii
cognitive learner, x-xiii
Google Books, xv
keyword, xi
kinesthetic learner, xiv
review, how to, xv
sample overview, xiv
semantic context, xii
visual learner, xiii
vocabulary, the
  importance of, ix

Words
abet, 18
abeyance, 19
abrogate, 20
abstruse, 21
alacrity, 22
amalgamate, 23
amiable, 24
anomaly, 25
apocryphal, 26
arbiter, 27
assiduous, 28
attenuation, 29
audacious, 30
aver, 31
baleful, 32
bane, 33
belie, 34
bellicose, 35
bemuse, 36
bereft, 37
bombastic, 44
boor, 45
broach, 46
cacophony, 47
candor, 48
capitulate, 49
capricious, 50
castigate, 51
chagrin, 52
cognizant, 53
conciliatory, 54
contumacious, 55
conundrum, 56
countermand, 57
craven, 58
credulous, 59
daunt, 60
debacle, 61
deleterious, 62
delineate, 63
demagogue, 70
demur, 71
denigration, 72
derision, 73
didactic, 74
diffidence, 75
dilatory, 76
discordant, 77
discursive, 78
disparage, 79
dogmatic, 80
dulcet, 81
duplicity, 82
eclectic, 83
efficacious, 84
effluvia, 85
effrontery, 86
embroil, 87
empirical, 88
encumber, 89
enervate, 96
enigma, 97
ephemeral, 98
epitome, 99
equivocal, 100
erudite, 101
esoteric, 102
evanescent, 103
evince, 104
exacerbate, 105
exculpate, 106
exhortation, 107
exonerate, 108
extenuating, 109
extricate, 110
fabricate, 111

fallacious, 112
fastidious, 113
fatuous, 114
feckless, 115
florid, 122
flout, 123
foment, 124
frenetic, 125
fulsome, 126
furtive, 127
garrulous, 128
gratuitous, 129
gregarious, 130
guile, 131
hapless, 132
hedonistic, 133
heretic, 134
hone, 135
impervious, 136
impetuous, 137
imprecation, 138
impute, 139
inane, 140
incongruous, 141
incursion, 148
indefatigable, 149
indolent, 150
indomitable, 151
ingenuous, 152
inimical, 153
innocuous, 154
insolvent, 155

intractable, 156
intransigence, 157
intrepid, 158
inure, 159
irascible, 160
lachrymose, 161
laconic, 162
lassitude, 163
lionize, 164
loquacious, 165
lugubrious, 166
maladroit, 167
malevolent, 174
melancholy, 175
mendicant, 176
mnemonic, 177
multifarious, 178
munificence, 179
nadir, 180
nascent, 181
nefarious, 182
obfuscate, 183
obsequious, 184
obstreperous, 185
officious, 186
opulent, 187
ossify, 188
palliate, 189
panegyric, 190
paradigm, 191
pariah, 192
parsimony, 193

paucity, 200
pellucid, 201
peregrination, 202
perfidious, 203
perfunctory, 204
pernicious, 205
petulant, 206
philanthropic, 207
phlegmatic, 208
piqu, 209
placat, 210
polemic/polemicist, 211
ponderous, 212
precipitous, 213
precocious, 214
predilection, 215
pretentious, 216
proclivity, 217
prodigious, 218
profuse/profusion, 219
prolific/proliferate, 226
prosaic, 227
protract, 228
provocation, 229
pundit, 230
purport, 231
quixotic, 232
raconteur, 233
ramify, 234
raucous, 235
reprobate, 236
reticent, 237

retrograde, 238
ribald, 239
sagacity, 240
salient, 241
salutary, 242
sanctimonious, 243
sanguine, 244
seminal, 245
sequester, 252
serendipity, 253
sophistry, 254
soporific, 255
stymie, 256
superfluous, 257
supersede, 258
surreptitious, 259
sycophant, 260
tawdry, 261
temerity, 262
tenacity, 263
transient, 264
truncate, 265
turpitude, 266
ungainly, 267
vacillate, 268
vapid, 269
voluble, 270
zealot, 271

Free Audio
ONLINE
http://solida.net/

VOCABBUSTERS

Make vocabulary **fun**, meaningful & memorable

study style

SOLID A

Dusti D. Howell, Ph.D.
Deanne Howell, M.S.
Copyright © 2005 Solid A, Inc.

www.ingramcontent.com/pod-product-compliance
Lightning Source LLC
Chambersburg PA
CBHW060457090426
42735CB00011B/2020